Twayne's United States Authors Series

EDITOR OF THIS VOLUME

David J. Nordloh
Indiana University

Oliver Wendell Holmes, Jr.

TUSAS 375

OLIVER WENDELL HOLMES, JR.

By DAVID H. BURTON

TWAYNE PUBLISHERS
A DIVISION OF G. K. HALL & CO., BOSTON

Library of Congress Cataloging in Publication Data

Burton, David Henry, 1925–
Oliver Wendell Holmes, Jr.

(Twayne's United States authors series ; TUSAS 375)
Bibliography: p. **161-65**
Includes index.
1. Holmes, Oliver Wendell, 1841–1935.
2. Judges—United States—Biography.
KF8745.H6B87   347.73′2634 [B]   80–10641
ISBN 0–8057–7262–6

Contents

About the Author

David H. Burton is a specialist in American intellectual history. He has published widely on Theodore Roosevelt, including a biography in the Twayne Rulers and Statesmen Series, as well as two special studies, *Theodore Roosevelt Confident Imperialist* and *Theodore Roosevelt and his English Correspondents*. *American History — British Historians*, which he brought out in 1976, was a Pulitzer Prize nomination book for that year. Besides articles on Holmes in the *Proceedings of the American Philosophical Society*, the *Harvard Library Bulletin* and *History Today* he has edited the *Holmes-Sheehan Correspondence* and *Oliver Wendell Holmes, Jr. What Manner of Liberal?*

Preface

This study of a complex mind, briefly examined, is an introduction to Oliver Wendell Holmes, Jr. It searches out Holmes in his legal and philosophical writings no less than in his court opinions. It proposes to build on the Holmes scholarship to date, and to draw on it as well: books by Bent, Biddle, and and Bowen, those two magisterial volumes by Mark deWolfe Howe which deal with Holmes's early life, commentaries by Frankfurter, Lerner, and Laski, collections of published correspondence, general histories of the Court and the Constitution, and particular treatments of those with whom Holmes associated. It is, in short, both a legal and a literary study.

Oliver Wendell Holmes was fond of saying that he defined truth as that in which he could not help but believe. This belief, furthermore, might have a variety of sources: history, experience, economic necessity, national advantage, common sense, or a gut feeling. Truth, like life itself, was mutable and unpredictable, and something about which men had disagreed and would continue to disagree. For Holmes, man was alone in the cosmos and had no choice but to make the best of his situation. A wise use of the law was one way he was able to cope with perplexity. For that reason man had developed legal codes, and for that reason they must be honored. This study argues, in consequence, that Holmes recognized his own contingency and what that implied; it follows his cosmic wanderings and renders his "can't helps" as a functional conscience. The book presents aspects of Holmes's life of the mind and pen well enough known but deserving fresh emphasis.

It also asks questions. Was Holmes liberal or conservative? Was he perhaps both liberal *and* conservative? Better still, are such labels simply irrelevant when applied to Holmes? Did Holmes not embrace certain absolutes of the heart while supporting a relativistic theory and application of the law? In the last analysis, was Holmes able to influence successive generations as well as his own because he helped to develop the principles of legal realism which he combined with a gift of expression? Was he a great judge because in part he was immensely quotable? His essays, his public addresses which quickly came into print, his great book, *The Common Law*, in addition to the memorable prose of many of his court opinions, entitle him to recognition as an American author.

Valuing Holmes as a public man who was also a man of letters is to place him alongside other Americans of like character. Benjamin Franklin's *Autobiography* merits attention no less than his statesmanship. John Adams's *Defence of the Constitutions of the United States* suggests that he was at least as good a writer as he was a president, while in the case of U. S. Grant's *Personal Memoirs* the literary man clearly eclipsed the political. Both Lincoln and John C. Calhoun exhibited rare literary gifts in the course of their public careers. John Hay, a secretary of state, moved from poetry to politics, while Theodore Roosevelt, characteristically, was simultaneously public man and man of letters. Holmes's historical reputation rests to some degree on his ability to convey the import of new legal principles in a variety of forms outside the law reports. Often remembered for his trenchant turn of phrase, Holmes should be regarded also for his enrichment of jurisprudential literature.

This identification of Holmes the legal authority and Holmes the author is a natural one and it reminds us that the thinker and the writer were one. He was, successively, student, attorney, scholar, teacher, and judge of the law. In each of these roles his reputation emerged, then solidified, and was finally preserved, because he was the author of a considerable body of works to which every student of Holmes must turn and upon which so much of the ensuing study rests.

This book is entirely of my own devising, whatever its merits or deficiencies. I must nonetheless thank a number of individuals who either have aided me or urged me on. Esmond Wright offered decisive encouragement in the formative stages of this work, and somewhere near mid-point William Harbaugh steadied my hand. To both I am grateful. It is appropriate to thank Charles J. Young, Vincent C. DeLiberato, and William E. Kirk for sharing some of their ideas on Holmes. What I have

Preface

made of their thoughts I can only hope they will approve. My colleague Graham Lee read early drafts of the study, saving it thereby from many a constitutional and legal misstep. As editor, David J. Nordloh improved both the focus and perspective which I brought to Holmes in history. Stephanie McKeller gave of her own time to help put the manuscript together. I must also thank the librarians and staffs of Saint Joseph's College Library and the Library of the Law School of Villanova University for many courtesies. Finally my work on this life of Oliver Wendell Holmes, Jr., has evoked memories of two well-remembered mentors Joseph T. Durkin, S.J., and the late Charles Callin Tansill. It is a privilege to dedicate this study to them.

DAVID H. BURTON

Chronology

tice Horace Gray as an associate justice of the Supreme Court of the United States.

1904 Dissents in the *Northern Securities* case.

1905 Dissents in the *Lochner* case; writes the majority opinion in *Swift and Company* v. *United States.*

1908 Dissents in the *Adair* v. *United States* and *First Employers' Liability* cases.

1909 Opinions begin to evince a Holmesian rather than either a liberal or conservative pattern.

1917 Reacts soberly to the entry of the United States into World War I, as new strains are placed on the Constitution.

1919 Writes the unanimous majority opinion in the *Schenck* case, wherein he elaborates the "clear and present danger" principle. Dissents in the *Abrams* case, rejecting the "bad tendency" principle of the majority.

1919– Acquires the reputation of a civil libertarian by views
1928 expressed in a variety of cases, including the *Milwaukee Social Democratic Publishing Company* v. *Burleson* (1920), *Gitlow* v. *New York* (1924), *Olmstead* v. *United States* (1927), and *United States* v. *Schwimmer* (1928).

1929 Fanny Holmes dies.

1932 Resigns as associate justice of the Supreme Court.

1935 Dies March 6, and is buried in Arlington National Cemetery, alongside his wife and among his comrades of the Twentieth Massachusetts Volunteer Infantry Regiment.

CHAPTER 1

The Shaping of Wendell Holmes

THE law was part of Oliver Wendell Holmes, Jr.'s, natural inheritance. Lawyers had been in the family at least from the time of the sixteenth century—Thomas Holmes of Gray's Inn— and judges, too, a maternal grandfather, Charles Jackson, having been a justice of the Supreme Judicial Court of Massachusetts. For his part, immediately upon completion of Civil War service, Holmes commenced his legal studies at Harvard and for the next seventy years, down to his death in 1935, his career never deviated from his commitment to understanding the meaning and usage of law. As a student, attorney, scholar, judge, Supreme Court justice, and elder legal statesman, Holmes came to value the law not as an abstruse exercise but as a living, vital aspect of American society. But Holmes, who was born in Boston on March 8, 1841, had a wider birthright than the law itself, however much in after years he was drawn to it. A world of thought, a native city of intellectual and moral preoccupation, a family diverse in learning and accomplishment, a father of wisdom widely proclaimed, all this and the total of its implications passed on to Wendell Holmes. By the time he had reached the age of twenty he had come to know who he was and what he was, though he was far less sure of what he wanted to become. If a number of elements associated with both "thinkers" and "doers" met in him, he was the richer for it. But the intersection of so many and varied strains, at the same time, made for a tension between father and son, between reality and the theory of law, between a conception of man and the cosmos—tensions which Holmes never completely exorcised and which in a unique way help to account for his distinctive place in the historical unfolding of law in America.

13

I *Inheritance*

Holmes's world of thought had roots in the Puritan mind. Just as John Cotton and his generation had sought to reconcile divine revelation with a thriving humanism, producing thereby an imposing if ephemeral Puritan synthesis, Holmes encountered a similar conflict between traditional attitudes and scientific imperatives in his study and uses of the law. No system builder, he nonetheless reflected his Puritan forebears in an earnest search for truth. Unable ultimately to capture that elusive commodity either in constitutional provision or in judicial opinion, Holmes was fated to remain an active philosopher-judge for all his years. He retained throughout an awe bordering on reverence for the "august Puritan figures" from the past. His own especial dedication to the law was the result of his Puritan temperament. For him "life was its own answer. He was a workman who found the stuff and patterns within himself, whose reward was their union."[1] Yet Holmes saw clearly that he had outgrown the Puritan faith, while valuing its legacy of earnest endeavor. "Even if our mode of expressing wonder, our awful fear, our abiding trust in the face of life and death, and the unfathomable world has changed, yet at this day, even now, we New Englanders are still leavened with the old Puritan ferment; our doctrines may have changed, but the cold Puritan passion is still here."[2] Such words as these, delivered on the occasion of an historic anniversary of the founding of the First Church in Cambridge, where his grandfather Abiel Holmes was once pastor, acknowledged his Puritan debt.

Because the Puritan beliefs had yielded to the frontier as well as to the new learning of the century of Enlightenment when Massachusetts grew from colony to province to state, Holmes came to respect eighteenth-century thought and to imbibe its revolutionary philosophy. American freedom was bred in his bones and one day he would answer a call to arms in defense of the Constitution and the Union, edifices built as much on ideas as on action. By the time Holmes was born, however, rationalism had been generously streaked with romanticism and reform was in the air. If America was to be true to its promise, it had to cleanse itself of slavery and a dozen other evils. Holmes as a young man surely was touched by such moral fervor which aimed at nothing less than a national rededication. He was a convinced abolitionist in the 1850s while at Harvard and viewed his Civil War enlistment in part as a commitment to the destruction of human slavery. But like his father, who refused to become either an abolitionist or a pacifist, he would remain aloof from causes and crusades once the passions unleashed by war had a chance to cool. Holmes was, in fact, a true Yankee, "torn between a passion for righteousness and a desire to get on in the world."[3] In the tension discoverable in his outlook, the distance between "is" and "ought" he kept manageable because of the eminently human faith and optimism of men like Ralph Waldo Emerson, whom he knew so well as a boy. Years later Holmes recounted to a friend how one day he met Emerson unexpectedly on the street and on impulse said to him, "If I ever do anything, I shall owe a great deal to you—which is true."[4] Whatever authority the new scientific postulates about the nature and the fate of man were to have on the developing mind of Holmes, the hopefulness of the reforming generation left a lasting mark on a nature which remained openly friendly to honor and sacrifice. "You and I," Holmes was to write to his close friend Sir Frederick Pollock years later, "believe that high-mindedness is not impossible to man."[5]

It requires no flight of imagination to visualize that meeting of Holmes, the boy, and Emerson, the mystic, on the streets of Boston. Boston was a city famous for its great men of philosophy and literature and every kind of learning. To happen on an Adams or a Longfellow or to glimpse Asa Gray or James Russell Lowell was typical of life in that holy place. It was the "hub of the universe," according to Holmes's phrase-making father, Dr. Holmes, "the Autocrat of the Breakfast Table," and the intellectual world revolved around it. Boston filtered the elements derived from the larger realms of thought beyond its boundaries. Not that the city gave its approval to certain beliefs only. The Boston mood could be open and expansive, albeit capable of parochialism and intellectual priggery of a high order if the occasion warranted it. Had not the Autocrat himself pronounced that Bostonians "all carry the Common in our heads as the unit of space, the State House as the standard of architecture, and

we measure off men in Edward Everetts as with a yardstick."
The Saturday Club, with its storied membership meeting monthly
at the Parker House, was the field for Boston's intellectual
jousts. Here ideas flowed as copiously as did the wine, and if
the results did not strictly add up to *in vino veritas*, the pursuit
and isolation of falsity in man, mind, and morals was a game
superbly played. To be detached and critical was a Boston
hallmark with which Holmes readily identified, though in his
years as a legal scholar and jurist he did not succumb as Boston
did to the complacent belief that his judgments were necessarily correct because he had uttered them.[6]

In the longer view Holmes would not feel comfortable as
Indian summer engulfed New England. His eye was fixed on a
farther, wider horizon, where Boston certainties might appear
as "a jingle of words with a jangle of contradictory meanings."[7]
Apart from such considerations of the mind, Boston was home to
Wendell Holmes. "I've always lived in Boston," was the terse
statement in his college autobiography for the Harvard Alumni
Album, a remark offered with the quiet pride of an Athenian of
old.[8] It was a town to be enjoyed for its houses and gardens, its
streets and architecture, its buildings reminders of a rich,
persuasive history, and all these things replete with a thousand
personal associations as well. It was a place to return to for
refreshment after days of battle or months of numbing fatigue
on the Supreme Court.

In that same sketch for the Harvard Album there is an apt
description of Holmes's family and his sense of it. "All my three
names," he wrote, "designate families from which I descended.
A long pedigree of Olivers and Wendells may be found in the
book called 'Memorials of the Dead—King's Chapel Burying
Ground.' . . . Some of my ancestors have fought in the revolution;
among the great grandmothers of the family were Dorothy
Quincy and Anne Bradstreet ('the tenth muse'); and so on. . . ."[9]
His earliest American forebear was one David Holmes, born in
England about 1635, died in Milton, Massachusetts, 1666. Within
a brief time the Holmes family became both plentiful and suc-
cessful. John Holmes, David's son and a surveyor of some skill,
built a sawmill and began accumulating land. John's son was
"Deacon" Holmes, and after him came another David, who was

a Revolutionary War officer, then the Rev. Abiel Holmes, a Yale man and a clergyman who was the father of Dr. Holmes and thus the grandsire of Wendell Holmes. The first Wendells were in America by 1640, coming out of Holland. On the Wendell side of the family Holmes was related to Wendell Phillips, Richard Henry Dana, and William Ellery Channing. Added to this, Wendell's father had married a second cousin, Amelia Jackson, giving the impression that the family was at once numerous, distinguished, and closely knit. Amelia Jackson's father, Judge Jackson, was a landowner who provided his daughter and son-in-law with their family house in Montgomery Place as a wedding gift, a successful businessman and a jurist. If the Holmes side of the family was noted for its learning with a dash of piety, the Jacksons introduced a preference for the practical which was to serve Wendell Holmes in good stead. Unlike his contemporary, young Henry Adams, Holmes grew up in Boston conscious of the place his ancestors had prepared for him in life and happy with the prospects. When in 1872 he married Fanny Bowditch Dixwell, the New England connection was complete. Fanny was the granddaughter of the well-known writer on navigation Nathaniel Bowditch; her father, E. S. Dixwell, a brilliant student two classes ahead of Dr. Holmes at Harvard, was a proper Boston schoolmaster. The wild streak in the Dixwell blood—it was said that John Dixwell had helped in the execution of Charles I—had been transmuted to a quiet *joie de vivre*, of which Fanny Bowditch Dixwell, luckily for Wendell Holmes, enjoyed a generous share.[10]

II *Father and Son*

Unlike many sons of a famous parent, Wendell Holmes managed to escape from the long shadow cast by his father. Indeed, unlike most children so favored, he came to exceed his parent in age and in historical reputation, if not in wisdom. But growing up under the roof as well as the shadow of the Autocrat was not a condition easily borne, despite the obvious advantages it entailed. The more Wendell learned the more he was likely to argue with his father and dissent in the bargain. If it is remembered further that Holmes brought his bride to his father's house and did not establish his own home until three years had passed, the opportunities for distemper between an egoistic father and his intellectually aggressive offspring must have been numerous. Wendell, anxious to go his own way, saw in his father's household presence, as in his household erudition, too much of what was intimidating and inhibiting. But the clash of two such self-confident personalities—including the possibility at least that in later years the younger Holmes took a special pleasure in the prospect of outstripping his father in the world of men and affairs—cannot disguise the influence which Dr. Holmes exerted on his eldest boy.[11] For one thing, freedom of thought in religious matters passed clearly enough from father to son. For another, it appeared to "observers of hereditary talent," that Holmes Jr.'s "subtle and original following out of analogies and the presentation of familiar elements in fresh lights" could be seen as derived on a straight line from Dr. Holmes.[12] More basic was the son's scientific attitude of mind: antimetaphysical, skeptical of development of constants and universals beneath the flux of change—all this learned at home far more so than at school. As Dr. Holmes was prone to view free will as illusory, substituting heredity and environment for Calvinistic predestination, Judge Holmes, for example, came to doubt the deterrent value of criminal punishment, holding that most criminal actions were but responses to stimuli. Wendell agreed unequivocally with his father that man's free will was often severely limited by chance circumstances and surroundings. Like his father he was dubious about the prospect of self-direction. Human frailty caused them both to question conventional concepts of moral responsibility. Though young Holmes found it uncongenial to confide in Dr. Holmes as to the origins and direction of his philosophical ideas, his broader frame of reference owed much to his father's scientific convictions. Nor for all of the irritants present in their relationship, real as they were but undoubtedly exaggerated with the retelling, should the natural affection of father and son be ignored. What may have been lacking in sentiment was made up for by admiration and respect.

The birth of Dr. Holmes's first son was for him an occasion of pride and promise. He wrote his sister, Ann, within hours of the event, describing the baby as "a little individual who may hereafter be addressed as ———— Holmes, Esq. or The Hon ———— Holmes, M. C. or His Excellency ———— Holmes, President."[13] Such hopes are perhaps no more common to men of distinction than to others, even though the air of confidence in Dr. Holmes's fancy was thoroughly consistent with his Brahmin mentality. By the age of six "o.w.h."—his father used this style of designating the little edition of O.W.H.—was attending a Dame's school and in the autumn of 1848 enrolled at a boys' academy run by a T. Russell Sullivan. The master was a former Unitarian minister who lost no occasion, whether the subject be the delivery of pure water to the city or the prospecting for gold in California, to invoke the name and the wonderful power of the Lord. After four years under Sullivan's tutelage, Holmes entered Dixwell's Private Latin School in Boylston Place, having impressed Master Sullivan with "habits of application," "proficiency in all the English branches," and a "love for study."[14]

III *School and Books*

Epes Sargent Dixwell, whose son-in-law Holmes was to become, had some claim to recognition as a classical scholar. Though he had read law and had engaged in a little practice, his true calling was that of schoolmaster. With an eye trained on the Harvard College entrance examination which stressed Latin, Greek, ancient history, and mathematics, Dixwell provided his charges with a solid grounding in these fundamentals. No narrow pedant himself, as his interest in conchology and membership in the Boston Society of Natural History testified, Dixwell saw to it that his students also read French and German and studied English as well as modern history, though these last-named subjects were approached with a good deal less intensity. Such formalities aside, Dixwell seems to have discovered in the young Holmes an apt companion for walks and talks after school as the two made their way home; and their friendship remained steadfast in the years to come.

In conjunction with schooling Holmes had an outlet for his budding literary tastes in the novels of Walter Scott—

Ivanhoe, Old Morality, and the *Fortune of Nigel*—as well as the writings of Dickens, Thackeray, Tennyson, and Macaulay. Lesser authors of the caliber of Mayne Reid, G. R. P. James, and Sylvanus Cobb, Jr., also offered Holmes stories of interest. Such boyhood enthusiasms as he displayed in reading Scott, for example, who was his favorite, provided a wholesome balance to the classical-language drills he daily faced at Dixwell's. Beyond school, and especially from his father and his mother, young Wendell learned the code of a humanized Christian ethic. Honor, courage, honesty, diligence, fidelity, while they all might be assumed, were nevertheless inculcated by precept not more than by example. But it was a practical morality Holmes tended to embrace as well as a highly personalized one, which even as a youngster he put to use. One of his recollections from childhood had to do with this practical brand of morality. Was it ever right to lie, he once asked his cousin and closest chum, John T. Morse, Jr., as the two boys were playing one day on Boston Common. When his companion answered "No," Holmes offered him a supposition. Suppose, he said, they were to see a man who, running toward them terrified of pursuers he knew to be close at his heels, bounded into a nearby thicket. Would it be wrong, queried Holmes, to deny to the pursuers any knowledge of the whereabouts of the man? Both boys concluded that it might be indeed the right and necessary thing to do in order to save the hare from the hounds.[15] In morality, as in the law, circumstances were known to alter cases.

Holmes was to survive three woundings during the Civil War, no little tribute to his good luck and to a certain physical toughness and resilience. As a youth he was not devoted to outdoor sports, and it was not until his army days that he learned to ride. Holmes is best thought of as a typical lad of his time. His greatest fun was sleighing on the hills of Boston. He also liked to row on the Charles, a pastime his father greatly encouraged. In 1849, when Wendell was about eight years old, Dr. Holmes built a summer house for the family near Pittsfield on land which had been in the family for generations. The site was on the Lenox Road and was called Canoe Meadows; it encompassed some 280 acres. Such a place was perfectly suited to children's holidaying, for by this time the Holmes family had expanded to include a sister, Amelia, and a brother, Edward. Here the children were free to fish and swim, pick berries, and explore the woodlands round about. This was the red-skin interlude for Wendell which schools introduce between the fast flowing tears of the child and the man: sitting at Xanthus-side amidst the camp fires or witnessing the battle in the West Country where Arthur fell. Holmes later spoke of these days as "my first recollections of the country—and what we love and revere is largely determined by our earliest memories."[16]

By his mid-teens Holmes had discovered a fresh and unusual outlet for his energies and his imagination. He had attained a feel for art and procured a set of etching tools and materials. Never minded to devote his life to drawing, this interlude proved great fun for him and at the same time diversified and enlarged his appreciation of the world about him. The knowledge he acquired of the techniques of woodcut, wood-engraving, and line-engraving was remarkable. Such drawings as he made were carefully done, proficient if not inspired; but he was shortly convinced that his efforts lacked "that final wiggle of genius.[17] Later, at Harvard, Holmes wrote a piece for the *Harvard Magazine*, "Notes on Albert Dürer," in which he sought to fuse his instinctive yen for art and his developing philosophical outlook. In fact his appreciation of art and artists remained a consistent part of him, though in later years he might be more prone to utilize his fondness for art to point up a larger moral observation. Addressing the Fiftieth Anniversary Dinner of his Harvard class in 1911, for example, he offered the thought: "Life is painting a picture, not doing a sum," one of those capsulized judgments with which he delighted his circle.[18]

Meanwhile Holmes also fed his spirit with more serious reading. Lamb's *Dramatic Poets* and *The Prometheus of Aeschylus* were books taken from library shelves to be read with evident satisfaction. Vaughan's *Hours with the Mystics* he pondered while still at Dixwell's, a book which he was later to tell Pollock constituted a "transit from boy to man."[19] And he had commenced a serious consideration of Plato which grew out of his course in Greek at school. Emerson—"Uncle Waldo," as Holmes affectionately knew him—had advice when Wendell confided to him that he was reading Plato: "You should read Plato at arm's length. Say to him: 'You have been pleasing the world for two thousand years; see whether you can please me.'"[20] Emerson's counsel appealed to him; his own critical awareness had begun to take shape and direction. He had clearly outgrown Dixwell's Private Latin School and was as ready as any of his age for entrance into Harvard College. His father might have said he was more ready than most of his fellow students. As it turned out, Harvard was to be a set of expectations, some fulfilled and some not, for O. W. Holmes, Jr., Class of '61.[21]

IV   *Harvard College*

The disappointments attending Holmes's years at Harvard (1857–1861) were born of incongruity; yet, paradoxically, this same incongruity enabled Holmes to forge for himself an inquiring and critical mind. He was no more trained to ask big questions or to challenge the traditional assumptions which governed the educational enterprise of Harvard College in the 1850s than were Master Dixwell's other graduates. Nor was he at first minded to do so. He made the transition from school to freshman year in college easily enough because the difference between the two was a matter not of a kind but of degree. By the close of his course of studies, however, he had become disenchanted with the limiting effect of indoctrination, recitation, and institutional discipline which summarized the educational life-style at Cambridge in those years. By formally and semiofficially seeking to deny Holmes (and to his fellow students as well) the spectrum of universal knowledge, by dismissing as insignificant Darwin's scientific findings, for example, the intellectual authority over her students which Harvard wished to exercise produced the reverse effect on Holmes. Like certain of his college friends, William James among them, Holmes wanted to twist the tail of the cosmos, and was not content to be the receptacle into which traditional morality and philosophical orthodoxy might be poured in carefully measured quantities. If Harvard was "an emphatic and unbuilding force in the life of Holmes," she taught her students, in Holmes's own phrase, "in ways not to be discovered, by traditions not to be written down, help[ing] men of lofty nature to make good their faculties."[22]

As Holmes's mind fleshed out, Harvard College proved less and less able to contain it. After a while he would no longer seek to conform, and for the last three years, with an increasing intensity, he agitated against the educational system.

The intellectual cross-purposes of institution and student notwithtanding, the total of Holmes's life at Harvard was not merely tolerable but pleasant to the point of enjoyable. As a freshman he took rooms at Mr. Danforth's on Linden Street, adjacent to but beyond the College Yard. He remained in residence there for his four years, thus avoiding the worst disciplinary features of dormitory life. All in all these arrangements provided more suitable an environment than living in college, giving Holmes a better chance to study, reflect, and write; he had come to Harvard seriously bent on learning. He was also active in the social clubs: the Institute, the Hasty Pudding, the Porcellian, and the Alpha Delta Phi. For a while at least he was a member of the Christian Union, an organization pointedly opposed to the highly orthodox and religiously rigorous Christian Brethren.[23] If little is known of the young collegian's social life beyond Harvard, in the drawing rooms of the best families of Boston and Cambridge, there is no reason to hold that the handsome and articulate son of Dr. Holmes lacked for female admirers. In his "Notes to account of my first wound," composed just after his first Civil War encounter at Ball's Bluff, he wrote: "While I was lying on the island, one of the thoughts that made it seem particularly hard to die was the recollection of several fair damsels whom I wasn't quite ready to leave."[24] Certainly he made close friends with fellow students. Norwood Penrose Hallowell, a Philadelphia Quaker who was to be the Orator of the Class of '61—as Holmes was Class Poet—was the best among them. Hallowell later served in the Twentieth Massachusetts Volunteer Infantry, Holmes's regiment, was wounded at Antietam, and remained a lifelong friend.

It would have been remarkable had young Holmes not strayed beyond the boundaries of College discipline and decorum as rigidly laid down and relentlessly enforced by the faculty, regulations which President Eliot in his 1869 inaugural address slightly referred to as "petty." Sanctions were placed on an endless list of indulgences large and small: smoking in the Yard,

missing chapel, breaking windows (something of an undergraduate obsession), blaspheming. The result was a state of
near-constant warfare between faculty and students. By living
off campus Holmes avoided conflict with a good many of these
rules, not that he was inclined to break them all. Rather his
resistance to the ways of Harvard was concerned more with
what he was taught, not with how he was to behave. As one
of the three senior editors of the *Harvard Magazine* he drew the
ire of President Felton when disrespectful language character-
izing a retiring professor found its way into the columns of the
magazine. On another occasion the faculty voted a public
admonition to Holmes for "repeated and gross indecorum in the
recitation of Professor Bowen."[25] Bowen's insistence on religious
orthodoxy as the one sound foundation for human behavior had
simply become too much for Holmes in his senior year. Given
the number of temptations a maturing, critical student must
have encountered along the way, the infrequency of penalties
levied against Holmes may be the more significant factor after
all for estimating his self-restraint. Such considerations, furthermore, may be best seen as unavoidable obstacles which simply
had to be overcome if students were "to make good their faculties." In the case of Holmes he made good the opportunity to
pass out of Harvard not merely as one experienced in protesting
against the system but as one equipped with a personal and
noble philosophy which, having fashioned it himself, became
part of him.

Wendell Holmes left a considerable record of his progress
along the paths of the learning and the intellectual independence for which he is well remembered. His sophomore essay,
"Books," is a useful early reference point. In its passages Holmes
insists that students must not be content with creeds which define all the possibilities and then say, "Thus far shall ye think,
and no farther." He contends, instead, that "we *must*, will we
or no, have every train of thought brought before us while
we are young. . . ."[26] This call for an intellect open to the universe was not, at so early a phase of his Harvard career, a hostile
reaction to the college's orthodoxies; the sentiments and convictions expressed in "Books" were matters of the Holmesian
temperament. He was, as he would remain, concerned with

"conclusions, or of such facts as enabled him to arrive at conclusions, on the great issues of right and wrong and on the relation of man to God." By calling for a life of the mind, as
opposed to a life taken up merely with events, Holmes argued
that books must be the starting point. Not alone the works of
Shakespeare, Montaigne, and Goethe, but Plato and Confucius,
and "the Buddhist and Zoroastrian sacred books" as well. As he
remarks in his essay, "books are but little seeds after all, seeming
insignificant before the merest weed of real life; but they lie
soaking in our minds and when we least expect it, they will
spring up, not weeds but supporters that will be our aid in the
sorest struggles of our life."[27] Behind the sententious prose of
the Harvard sophomore Holmes's mind was beginning to coil.
It would draw together tighter and tighter over the course of his
schooling before and after the Civil War, set to spring loose
upon the law as upon all of life.

The case for books having been amply stated, what books in
particular appear to have absorbed Holmes's energies in these
years, apart from college texts like Bowen's *The Principles of
Metaphysical and Ethical Science Applied to the Evidences of
Religion* and Thomson's *Law of Thought* which were typical of
the standard reading in most courses he took? Plato's *Dialogues*
was a constant companion. He also studied Fichte's *Contribution to Mental Philosophy*, contemplated Butler's *Ancient Philosophy* and Cousin's *Modern Philosophy*, and returned again and
again to Vaughan's *Hours with the Mystics*. The ongoing struggle
to fashion his own peculiar intellectual outlook, and the drift
of that outlook away from traditional, orthodox moorings was
evident in his reading of Lowes's volumes *Comte's Philosophy
of the Sciences* and *Biographical History of Philosophy*. These
latter books no doubt helped to polarize Holmes's thinking on
the methods of truth-seeking and the possibilities of truth-finding
without, in the end, convincing him of the logical positivist's
confident dismissal of all that can not be seen and measured as
irrelevant.

Holmes became one of those thinkers who quite frankly and
firmly insisted on reading philosophy from the point where he
stood in historical time backward to the ancient Greeks. ". . . I
regard pretty much everything, and especially the greatest

things, in the way of books, as dead in fifty, nowadays in twenty years." he told one friend in 1909. "The seeds of thought germinate and produce later seeds. The old structures are remodeled and have electric lights put in." He then went on to describe himself as one who "thinks that Philosophy and the philosophy of history really have advanced within recent times...."[28] In light of these assertations, the formative potentiality of his Harvard years is registered unmistakably in an essay, "Plato," which he published in the October 1860 issue of the *University Quarterly*, an intercollegiate journal of undergraduate opinion. Following the advice of Emerson not to accept Plato's philosophy unless, in fact, Plato pleased him, Holmes undertook to apply his growing skepticism to some of Plato's favorite generalizations. "Man is man, again Plato also says, just as far as he partakes of humanity. . . . But here, as it seems to me, there is a serious confusion introduced ... owing to the admitting equally, without distinction, the simple ideas like those in which mathematical truth is dependent . . . and those like humanity, which is a purely general statement. In other words, as long as we have faith in reason we must believe in the truths of mathematics ... while we see at least no such necessary existence for the ideas of humanity, etc." Holmes discovers an "unhappy fallacy" in Plato in that he confounded conclusions present in logic with conclusions drawn from new data. Admitting that Plato's philosophy is a "vast step" in introducing more accurate and well defined thought than had previously existed, "it still needed a complete remodeling before it would suffice as a consistent cosmology." "Our chemists do know more really than the best of the alchymists ... and so with ancient metephysics." For Holmes "we start far beyond the place where Plato rested." Nevertheless, there is in this essay a lingering regard for the "intuitive faculty" in man which makes the position of its author a trifle ambiguous. His quarrel is not so much with Plato as a thinker but with those who continued to quote Plato, oblivious to the rise of science which rendered Plato, not useless, but anachronistic. Plato's value to the philosopher is still real; seeing "a really great and humane spirit fighting the same fight as we ourselves" was inspiring.[29] Yet Plato's answers were, in the main, out of date. No less a philosopher than Emerson had read this essay on Plato in draft form. "I have read your piece," he told the young Holmes. "When you strike at a king, you must *kill* him."[30] Yet for Holmes and his intellectual world the time was not yet ripe for dismissing Plato and his answers altogether. He could still talk sincerely of coming to know the "necessary ideas" which are part of the "mind of the Creator," while trusting more in science than in intuition.[31]

"Notes on Albert Dürer," which Holmes wrote over the summer months of 1860, showed a similar propensity.[32] Dürer's treatment of religious subjects attracted him because his drawing technique appealed to the draughtsman in him and because contemplation of the artist's work yielded meaning for him. It was the mood which Dürer was able to evoke—the ultimately tragic fate of mankind—and not so much the religious message of the pictures which fascinated him. Indeed, in this essay, Holmes is prepared to say that Dürer, like Plato, had become outdated if one sees only and even primarily the message of salvation. "The growth of civilization increases our faith in the natural man and must accordingly detract from the intense and paramount importance attached in darker times to the form of the story embodying the popular religion." Yet Holmes's attraction to Dürer's drawings, with their unavoidable overtones of religious spirituality, remains unexplained, save by his temperamental need to fathom the fullest meaning of man which itself tends to suggest a residual belief, or faith in God. Unable to accept the faith of an age that was passed, he was not ready to take "the leap into the dark" on the reassurances of science. And so he focused in his "Notes on Albert Dürer" on man himself. His description of Dürer's *Meloncolia* spoke something of his youthful anguish. "That solitary picture is the true picture of his [man's] soul, in its strength and its weakness; powerful, but half overcome by the many objects of its universal study; crowned with the wreath of the elect and beautiful with an ideal genius, but grave with thought and marked with the care of the world; winged, yet resting sadly on earth."[33] That the art and thought of Dürer appealed to Holmes for more than half a century is clear from a 1923 letter in which he wrote of his collection of Dürer engravings and woodcuts, many of them having been in his possession since the Civil War. The consistent tension which is discoverable in the whole range of Holmes's life of the mind is traceable in some part to the impressions made by Dürer's work, which itself seemed to want to suspend judgment between God and man, Heaven and hell.

V *Call to Arms*

Wendell Holmes's final term at Harvard was an unsettled one. The imposition by orthodox professors of principles of metaphysics and *laissez-faire* economics was but part of the discontent. The Civil War was bearing down on Harvard men no less than on other Americans, and Holmes was caught up in these great events which led on to strife. Wendell Phillips had once again stirred Boston in favor of the cause of abolition. Lincoln's call for volunteers to put down the Southern rebellion broke the spell of uncertainty and indecision which hung across the land. Holmes was, for the moment at least, an abolitionist. Within two weeks of the presidential proclamation of April 15, 1861, he had enlisted as a private soldier in the Fourth Battalion of the state militia and had commenced training at Fort Independence in Boston Harbor. Harvard College was suddenly remote. Once it was clear that the Fourth Battalion was not slated for immediate action, both Holmes and his father had some sober second thoughts about the college career which was so near successful completion. It was possible for him to remain in military service and yet take the examinations for his degree. The willingness of the faculty to accept him back on these terms, the fact that he had already been elected Class Poet, and the time required for his application for a commission to be processed all conspired to enable Holmes to graduate Harvard with the Class of 1861. Then, on July 23, 1861, within a week of commencement exercises, Oliver Wendell Holmes, Jr., aged twenty, was commissioned a lieutenant and joined A Company, Twentieth Massachusetts Volunteer Infantry. The Civil War awaited him.

VI *Lessons of War*

The transition from peace to war was a swift and painful one for Wendell Holmes. Commissioned in July 1861 and ordered

South with his regiment in September, he was wounded the next month in the battle of Ball's Bluff. "Hit in the beginning of the fight," he wrote his mother from a military hospital two days later, to which he added hopefully, "we'll lick 'em yet though."[34] Such were the ways during the first months of the Civil War: raw recruits led by unseasoned officers with heavy casualties the usual result—as Holmes's own experience testifies. Commission in hand and with little enough training, he was expected to lead troops, green and feckless youth for the most part drawn from New England farms and villages, into battle. As dangerous as such a situation was to the soldiers in the ranks, it was both hazardous and harrowing for the junior officers who had to assume responsibility for leadership while facing the same risk of death as the men under their command. Nothing that Wendell Holmes had known in life had prepared him for this ordeal. But perhaps Harvard had helped to ready his response. At college he had worked hard to refine a "noble philosophy" in which he could truly believe and by which, in consequence, he could guide his behavior. Battle would be the first, and possibly the supreme, test of that philosophy.

Like all citizen-soldiers Holmes was to learn by doing and, perchance, by dying—the lot of "the infantry of the line [which] stood the great slaughter."[35] The three separate wounds he received, at Antietam, September 1862, and at Fredericksburg, May 1863, in addition to Ball's Bluff, October 1861, are reminders of how constant was the danger to life itself, how often luck or fate played a part in survival. Nor was Holmes indifferent to such considerations. "My Dear Parents," he wrote just after being hit at Antietam, "Once more I back it as per hint of yesterday's letter—Usual luck—ball entered at the rear passing through the central seem of coat & waistcoat collar coming out to the front of the left side. . . ." Luck today; fate tomorrow: "now as ever I believe that whatever shall happen is best."[36] And so the war came to Wendell Holmes.

For every soldier who survives the ravages of battle there must always remain two wars: the war in fact and the war in memory. But more rare is the veteran who displays a peculiar need to recall battles, toast old wounds years afterwards, relive personal tragedies, and commemorate great events and great

friends as did Holmes. In consequence he tended to impart a
patina of unreality to the horrors he spoke and wrote of, once
he was *hors de combat*. Perhaps it was only an effort to cast out
the devils which are war's daily companions and which continue to haunt old soldiers despite the years. The evidence that
he reflected on the war and its lessons is overwhelming. In writing to Frederick E. Pollock he noted: "I always think that when
a man has once had his chance—has reached the table land over
his difficulties—it does not matter much whether he has more
or less time allowed him in that stage. The real anguish is
never to have your opportunity. I used to think that a good
deal during the war."[37] And he told Harold Laski, one of his
confidants, more than half a century after Appomattox, "The
army taught me some great lessons—to be prepared for catas-
trophe—to endure being bored—and to know that however fine
a fellow I thought myself in my usual routine, there were other
situations alongside and many more in which I was inferior to
men that I might have looked down upon had not experience
taught me to look up."[38]

Other equally serious and far-reaching lessons he learned
as well. The three distinctive elements which stand out in
Holmes's reaction to the Civil War are strikingly alike com-
ponents discernible in his later intellectual growth. Soldiering
did not thwart so much as it nurtured that development in
altogether novel ways. Holmes came to treat the duties and the
dangers of war pragmatically. He learned by doing and readily
saw, at peril to his life, that old habits might have to be
discarded and new skills acquired if military success was to be
achieved. His ability to adapt was proven regularly in battle.
Success was tantamount to survival. What contributed to survival in one situation might have to be avoided in another, as the
demands of the engagements shifted. Beyond these everyday considerations, men like Holmes viewed the war as a matter of
efficiency versus inefficiency. They thought of winning the war
in practical, pragmatic terms, rather than according to the
enthusiasms of the home front. Duty for them could depend
"less in relation to great causes and more as a matter of doing
the necessary tasks in an efficient way."[39] Individual survival

and military success were linked to the least wasteful and quickest methods of victory.

Whatever the ingredient of luck, soldiers in action feel, as Holmes felt, that survival is bound up with the will to struggle, the will to survive, perhaps bound up even with the momentary illusion of immortality in this life. To the soldier who continues to function as a human being, and Holmes for all his exposure to brutality remained intensely human, war does not appear as it might seem to the generals—that is, an awesome use of lives to gain an objective. It is more intimately involved with an individual's desire to stay alive, however reckless or selfless his behavior under fire. Viewed from without war is an inexorable mechanism for destruction; but from within it is each individual's determination not to be destroyed. There is discoverable in any battle condition, and in the larger context of war, a curious blending of pragmatic and social Darwinist elements which for Holmes worked themselves out under circumstances certain to leave a lasting impression.

The cause which made Holmes's struggle against extinction and his pragmatic response to survival appeal to him as worthwhile comes through as a reminder that, at this stage in his growth, tradition and traditional values could have an almost decisive place. There was no pressing need on his part to enlist in the Union Army; no special social stigma attached to those young men of his generation who did not enlist. While a great many Harvard graduates did join the fight, not a few of his social class—and the young Henry Adams and William Everett come to mind—did not. Those who shunned military duty were not stirred by the same noble impulse which stirred Wendell Holmes. If his service was an expression of a youthful rebellion against parental and institutional authority, his avowed purpose, to help in the destruction of slavery, placed his decision in a context of values. Beyond that we may be sure that Holmes's response to the presidential call for volunteers was patriotic in a direct and ennobling way. Lacking the social compulsion to enter the army, there was a compelling Puritan sense of duty to be performed. The call to arms came not alone from Lincoln but from across the years, across the generations of Puritan forebears. Giving an account of his conduct at Ball's Bluff, Holmes

saw himself as acting "very cool and did my duty I am sure."[40]
On another occasion he described himself as 'heartily tired and
half worn out body and mind by this life, but I believe I am
as ready as ever to do my duty."[41] Evidence from Holmes's record
of service bears out the primacy of duty in his set of working
values.

The concept of duty figured throughout Holmes's wartime
letters and diary and was registered in his postwar reflections.
In his Memorial Day Address at Keene, New Hampshire, May
30, 1884, he praised the duty he judged his own to be in
celebrating the sacrifice of his intimate friend Henry L. Abbott,
killed at Cedar Montain, August 1862. Of Abbott Holmes said,
"He was indeed a Puritan in all his virtues without a Puritan
austerity; for when duty was at an end he who would have
been master and leader became the chosen companion in every
pleasure a man might honestly enjoy. In action he was sublime."[42]
Even as Holmes was nearing the end of his enlistment and found
himself thoroughly whipped by the war, duty remained paramount. "I honestly think that the duty of fighting has ceased
for me," he wrote his mother in June of 1864, "ceased because
I have laboriously and with much suffering of mind and body
earned the right . . . to decide for myself how I can best do my
duty to myself, to the country, and, if you choose, to God."[43]
In like vein he told Charles Eliot Norton about the same time:
"If one did not believe this war was a crusade in the cause of
the whole Christian world it would be hard to keep the hand to
the sword."[44] Such thoughts as these coming at the end of
Holmes's long trial as a soldier expose the deep roots of conviction regarding the war. Furthermore, the acknowledgment
of absolute values in his scheme of living helps to delineate his
traditionalism. Later intellectual adventuring would supply
rationales for pragmatic adaptation and struggle for survival
which battlefield experience had woven into his subconscious.
No such philosophical justification for the absolute demands
of duty and loyalty would be forthcoming, however, so that
Holmes's reasons for making the sacrifices attendant to the
war would remain the same reason which enabled him, some
thirty years afterward, to praise as "true and adorable that
which leads a soldier to throw away his life in obedience to

a blindly accepted duty. . . ."[45] Uncertain of the meaning of the universe, the demands of duty remained absolute. If remembrance of battles past was the only consideration causing the mature Holmes to proclaim a belief in absolutes, that in itself is some measure of the impact of the Civil War on the young Boston aristocrat who was so eager to join the fight in 1861.

VII   *War's Lasting Effects*

Years after the event, Holmes advised one friend that since "the Civil War the world never seemed quite right again."[46] His insistence upon such a judgment demands a careful assessment of the particular ways in which he had been changed by his wartime experiences, or at least what evolving characteristics of mind and faith found nourishment or possibly confirmation in the agonies of battle. Traits of the mature Holmes are easily related to the war, traits ambivalent in a revealing fashion. Aristocratic, yet democratic; detached, but involved; stoic while passionate; callous, though tender; convinced of life as a quaint adventure of the protoplasm without losing sight of man's innate dignity—these were the contradictions which distinguished the impact of the Civil War on Wendell Holmes.

Holmes had volunteered in 1861 out of an aristocratic sense of responsibility which was part of his New England birthright. Duty to him was inbred rather than deliberated. Yet the Civil War stripped away the artificialities of social rank by throwing individuals back on their own resources, as Holmes came quickly to appreciate. His first sergeant, when he commanded G Company, was Gustave Magnitzky, an immigrant newly arrived from Polish Prussia. Holmes's estimate of Magnitzky was the description of a natural aristocrat: "quiet and steady under fire, quiet and effective in camp, modest, distinguished in bearing and soul. . . ."[47] He was prepared to give him rank equal to that of an Abbott or a Hallowell in the company of soldiers and gentlemen. Wendell's democracy was the equal of his aristocratic sense.

It has been argued to good effect that the war promoted in Holmes his Olympian detachment in the face of a war, or a world, calling for answers to unanswerable questions.[48] Further-

more, he himself once conceded that "in the Civil War I formu-
lated to myself the value of prejudice and being cocksure for
achievement."[49] Some of the very passages from his wartime
letters which underscore his sangfroid are interlaced, however,
with Holmes's frustration at not being able to stop the loss
of life which he was witness to. "It is odd how indifferent one
gets to the sight of death—perhaps, because one gets aristocratic and don't [sic] value much a common life—Then they are
apt to be so dirty it seems natural—'Dust to Dust'—I would do
anything that lay in my power but it doesn't much offset my
feelings."[50] Similar evidence shows how the stoic remained
the passionate young man. Having announced his decision to
leave the army: "so I mean to leave at the end of the campaign
as I said, if I am not killed before," in the same letter he
described "the intense yearning" for "home and parents" which
he said immediately precedes a campaign.[51]

The toughness of the mature Holmes is axiomatic. "I believe
that force is the ultimate ratio" and "three generations of im-
beciles are enough" are vintage Holmes. Such views no doubt
found a source in the horrors of the war so often recalled. He
could speak with callous measure of heavy battle losses as "the
butcher's bill" at a point when the war was "kill-kill all the
time." Yet he did not descend to the brutish level. "A thousand
loving thoughts this Sunday Morng [sic]." "Day beautiful
and quiet," "Love to all" are phrases common in his letters and
diary during those days when he was his most disdainful of
life. His soul-searching over the decision to be mustered out
of the army arose from the inner thoughts of a person who continued to weigh his behavior in a human scale of values.

Holmes's doubts about his meaning in the cosmos subsequent
to his first wound—"Would the complex forces which made a
still more complex unit in *ME* resolve themselves back into
simpler forms or would my angel be still winging his way onward
when eternities had passed?"[52]—soon gave way to his own
peculiar agnosticism. This is not the same as saying that life was
futile. The Civil War taught Holmes that life had a worth in
itself, that there was an ineffable value to battles fought, and
better still, to battles won, a quality which lent dignity and
carried within it its own purpose. It will not do to draw from

Holmes's oft-quoted remarks in speeches long after the events, including the famous "Soldiers' Faith." Better to listen to the man at arms who took sure if quiet pride in soldiering and especially in his regiment. "I really very much doubt whether there is any Regt, wh. can compare with ours in the Army of the Potomac. Everyone says this who belongs to a good Regt. but still I fancy I am right from the evidence of many things."[53] In his regiment Holmes had a mirror for his own sense of devotion to duty and accomplishment. The regiment became his "beloved 20th." It identified him positively with something outside himself, something he believed in and was intensely loyal to. By giving loyalty to an absolute, namely, the unyielding principle of duty, Holmes verified the truth of that principle. In his own later phrase, truth is what I "can't help" believe. Coming at a time when such lessons were indelibly written, Wendell Holmes left the war touched not alone by fire but by the spirit of man's strange and perplexing purpose.

CHAPTER 2

Holmes and the Law

I Soldier's Return

WENDELL Holmes's war with the Rebels ended in the summer of 1864, and his war with the Autocrat resumed almost at the same time. Though the two often had disagreed about the purpose of the Civil War and the political and military methods employed in the bloody struggle, Wendell was, after all, the soldier whose experience and understanding of battle, of victory and defeat, gave him an exceptional authority to speak. Even the Doctor could be moved to silence on this account. But now the scene had changed, reverting to something like the old father-and-son relationship. As it became increasingly evident in the late summer of 1864 that the Union would prevail in the armed contest—though no man yet was prepared to speak of the final costs—Wendell's personal future took precedence over Lincoln's decisions and Grant's tactics in discussions which arose between Wendell and Dr. Holmes. Those discussions and that future revolved around Wendell's apparent preference for law as his life's work.[1]

As early as 1861 Holmes had written in his Harvard Class Book of an intention to study law as a profession if he survived the war, law "at least as a starting point."[2] He also indicated as much in his army identification papers, wherein he described himself as a law student.[3] His grandfather Jackson, of course, had been lawyer and judge, while his father's brother, Uncle John, read law and practiced a little at the bar. Indeed, Dr. Holmes himself had had a brief bout with legal study before turning to medicine and other diversions. Furthermore, law was an honorable calling and might just prove to be lucrative—not irrelevant considerations for a young man, without great expectations, who was determined to make his own way in the world while leaving his mark on it.

Still, the Autocrat raised some objections, at least at first. "A lawyer can't be a great man," he told Wendell when the latter announced his intention of entering Harvard Law School.[4] It was the kind of verbal shaft the senior Holmes could so deftly employ, and it had the usual effect on his son: deflating and challenging at the same time. But Dr. Holmes's choice of words was also revealing. He did not say: "Wendell, you can't be a great man as a lawyer," but only that "a lawyer can't be a great man." Dr. Holmes's objection was a matter of temperament, his temperament, and not a basic conviction that Wendell could not achieve greatness. Wendell was, after all, flesh of his flesh and that counted for something. This temperamental rejection of the law he chose often to register in quips. "If you can eat sawdust without butter you will be a success in the law" and "If you would wax thin and savage like a half fed spider, be a lawyer" were two of his favorites.[5] Beyond that, the Autocrat had a disdain for what he discovered to be the stock in trade of lawyers, the obfuscation of principles to perpetrate injustices. The law was all very intellectually demeaning.

Such objections Wendell Holmes, aged twenty-three, veteran of the Civil War, brevetted lieutenant colonel, could have dismissed readily except for his own inner doubts. The future record is suggestive. Holmes was not a great success as a practicing attorney; he found the legal routine dull and was not much attracted to client relations. His career at Harvard was too limited to give more than a hint that he might have developed into a great teacher. In contrast, work as editor on the *American Law Review* revealed a probing mind, well furnished to question and criticize, his researches in bringing out a new edition of *Kent's Commentaries* were a monument to his diligence as a scholar, and his famous book, *The Common Law*, established his reputation as a legal thinker of the first rank. If Holmes pondered his choice of a career, if he consulted Emerson and Uncle John, he hesitated out of respect for his penchant for the speculative: to contemplate the unanswered (and perhaps unanswerable) questions. Should he read philosophy, go to

England or to the Continent? Some of the men he most respected, William James, Charles Peirce, and Chauncey Wright,
were for it. And after that there could be a faculty appointment
at Harvard, an admirable vantage point for taking on the
cosmos. Much of his undergraduate education had shown a
taste for the philosophers; his reading drifted naturally in their
favor. He felt comfortable, at ease with them. When he seemed
to move in such a direction the Autocrat viewed the study of
law in a more appealing light, because it was a practical endeavor. Dr. Holmes, the man of science, did not entertain
much optimism for the prospects of "speculation." Despairing
of his namesake as a natural scientist, the father, as Holmes
later was to remark, "put on the screws to have me go to the
Law School—I mean he exerted the coercion of the authority
of his judgment." With such circumstances in mind Holmes
was to recall that he had been kicked into the law.[7]

Ultimately, however, Holmes, and Holmes alone, made the
decision to study law, remaining faithful to it over the course
of many years. Why? Because of the Autocrat's challenge? Because the law was tangible in a way that suited him, "more
immediately concerned with the highest interests of man than
any other [branch of knowledge] which deals with practical
affairs"?[8] Because academic life would be only half a life, too
far removed from the action for one who had heard the roar of
battle? Because Holmes discerned, at least faintly, that law
could "furnish philosophical food to philosophical minds"?[9]
Because the law offered a better chance for an income adequate
to one who did not choose to spurn pleasantries of society? All
these motives in some unfathomable combination—and perhaps
others as well—figured in his decision. For Wendell Holmes in
September of 1864, to study law seemed the thing to do.

II *Harvard Law School*

Contrasts between the highly regimented life of Harvard
College as Holmes might have recalled it from the prewar days
and the nonchalance of the Law School, which he entered that
fall, could not have been lost upon him. Though the faculty
recommended a certain sequence of courses to be taken, the

courses students actually enrolled in remained a matter of choice if not convenience. Attendance at lectures was not required, and Holmes for one did not even enroll for the 1866 spring term, preferring to pursue his training in the law offices of Robert Morse. Finally, no written examination was prescribed to qualify for the LL.B. degree, a condition which was not altered until 1870 when President Eliot installed Christopher Columbus Langdell as Law School dean. Since it was Langdell who first introduced the case method at Harvard, Holmes was not to benefit from this innovative and highly successful approach to the study of law. He and his fellow students attended lectures by Professors Parker, Parsons, and Washburn—these three constituted the sum total of the full time Law faculty at the time—the purpose of which was to explicate legal principles already established. As for legal principles in the making, wherein lay the great merit of the case method, such a concept was alien to their intellectual disposition. Beyond the lectures—and the evidence suggests that Holmes was in faithful attendance until being invited by Morse to enter his office—the student was expected to undertake a good deal of reading. Austin's *Principles of Jurisprudence* and Walker's *Introduction to American Law,* books of an historical and even philosophical cast, were typical, along with such standard treatises as Greenleaf on Evidence and Parsons on Contracts. Treatments like those of Austin and Walker were bound to give the reader a feel for the larger outlines of the law, that sense of history which the case method standing by itself failed to convey.

As it was for the practice of law that the school promised to prepare its students—"Harvard Law School was conducted very much like a lawyer's office"[10]—the moot court became an important component of the curriculum. Two such courts flourished in Holmes's day, one under the auspices of the faculty and another conducted by the students of the Marshall Club. Wendell Holmes was a notorious "talker," so moot court proceedings appealed to him immensely. Living as he was in his father's house in Charles Street, he often carried the arguments home, filling the household air with his version of the mock trials. Slowly, perhaps, but unmistakably, his enthusiasm for what he was about meant that Wendell Holmes was settling into the law.

More important than talking like a lawyer, he was beginning to
think like one, beginning to find himself at home. Not that he
was necessarily satisfied, even at this early date, with the state
of things as he discovered it, the law ladened with tradition and
seemingly fixed. "The law is not a brooding omnipresence in
the sky," as he later remarked, "but the articulate voice of some
sovereign or semi-sovereign that can be identified."[11] Before
long he would be eager to identify the sovereign, to probe the
source of law, and to do so in the rising spirit of the scientific
times in which he lived.

The legal profession when Holmes entered Harvard Law
School stood on the threshold of the modern phase of its development. After a golden age of revolutionary jurisprudence,
which lasted until the new constitutional government had
proved its operational worth, the profession came under heavy
pressure during the years of Jacksonian democracy. It had to
struggle against a democratic onslaught in order to remain a
force in American society. It did so by acknowledging that
though law was a rational science whose basic principles could
be easily grasped by all men, uncertainties were likely to arise
when principles were applied to different factual situations.
Success for a lawyer was thus bound up with common sense
and firsthand awareness of daily practicalities, while at the same
time a study of law as a subject was needed in order to fit theory
to practice. The best lawyer was a self-made one, in keeping
with the democratic requirements of the age and the Protestant
ethic of "work and win." Added to this was a growing concern
that law and politics should go separate ways. Finally, and perhaps not incidentally, successful lawyers gained appropriate
pecuniary rewards. Lawyers were gentlemen and should live
in a becoming style. All these elements, part of the self-image
of the American lawyer down to 1860, are readily discernible
in the legal outlook of Oliver Wendell Holmes, suggesting the
influences of this self-image of the legal profession during his
youthful, formative years.[12]

III   England and the Continent

The temptation is to think of Holmes connected to the law

by a straight line, possessed of a direct and consuming commitment to things legal. By temperament and training he did, in
fact, enter fully into whatever particular matter concerned him
at a given time: Latin verbs at Dixwell's, Plato at Harvard, duty
in war, accomplishment in legal training. But Wendell Holmes
was no mere compulsive, however worthwhile the purpose of
his various endeavors. Many windows had opened upon the
world while he was growing up in his father's house, windows
with views far afield from America and farther still from Boston.
The Autocrat had studied medicine in Paris, he was well known
and widely appreciated in England for his wit and humor. He
believed that Wendell must have a set of like experiences, and
was eager for him to go abroad once the Civil War had been
won. He wanted him to meet important people in England and
gain from them stimulation which, reciprocated over the years,
would be a valuable additive to his outlook. As Wendell was
planning his Old World visit for the summer of 1866, Dr. Holmes
procured a letter of introduction for him from John Lothrop
Motley to John Stuart Mill. In requesting it, he described his
offspring as a "presentable youth with fair antecedents, and is
more familiar with Mill's writings than most fellows of his
years."[13] Such formalities apart, invitations would come readily
enough. The younger Holmes already knew Leslie Stephen,
whom he met in Boston while recovering from his third wound,
and they had liked each other at once. Through Stephen he
would meet, among others, the latter's older brother Fitzjames
Stephen, a legal scholar of repute, and Thomas Hughes, the
author and moralist. John Stuart Mill introduced him to John
Elliott Cairnes, whose book *The Slave Power* he had read in
army camp. In addition, he spoke with Gladstone, who impressed
him very much. On a trip to Oxford, Holmes talked with Gold-
win Smith and breakfasted with the Master of Balliol himself,
Benjamin Jowett. This was a dazzling array of people, person-
ages, and personalities for a young man of twenty-five to encounter on so brief a visit.

His English interlude contributed to a growing maturity. He
was invariably the youngest in his constantly changing circle
of friends, and a foreigner besides, about whom people were
more rather than less curious. Relishing the role of an American

abroad, Holmes nonetheless felt completely sympathetic to the tone of the English intelligentsia, drawn to it by the magnet of a mutual fondness for learning. His already established interest in the law was good reason for him to think in Anglo-American terms. Apart from the law, he felt a "sympathy of comprehension" between America and England, well demonstrated by his later friendship with Englishmen as dissimilar as Sir Frederick E. Pollock and Harold Laski.

Holmes used the summer of 1866 to visit Europe as well as the British Isles. Of necessity he must see Paris: the house and the street where his father had lived during his medical student days; the Louvre, where his artistic instincts could command an immense variety of subjects for scrutiny and reflection; the city itself, with the woods, parks, bridges, and vistas of a Paris which had been born again. As he had agreed to do some mountain climbing with Leslie Stephen, he went to Basle after two weeks in France. The climbing was the most strenuous and the most dangerous thing he had done since his army experience, and his brief stint of mountaineering sealed his bond of friendship with Stephen. Holmes was happy to be back in England by the end of July with renewed opportunities to enjoy the English countryside and the Scottish Highlands and a solemn visit to Stratford-upon-Avon thrown in.

It would be impossible to attempt to sum up the significance of these four months abroad. Too many associations were made which would sustain him, too many seedlings of ideas planted which would come to fruition in the years to come. He returned to America in September with a renewed concern for his legal career. Yet his voyaging suggests that the connection between Holmes and the law cannot be visualized as running on a straight line. If, as he was wont to say, "a page of history is worth a volume of logic,"[14] then with equal purpose it may be asserted that the first experience of England was worth volumes of its history. Beyond introduction to some important thinkers, Holmes did not profit directly or immediately from these months away. But inasmuch as the Common Law was woven from the materials of English history, his enhanced awareness of things English quietly occupied a prominent place in his outlook.

IV *Litigating Lawyer*

Back in Boston, Holmes resumed his legal studies with a view to admission to the bar of Massachusetts. Though he had received an LL.B. from Harvard in June, he continued to prepare for his bar examination in the offices of one of the city's important firms, Chandler, Shattuck, and Thayer. This was a "litigating" partnership, so that Holmes was quickly exposed to the life and the rhythm of practicing court attorneys. He could have received no better preparation anywhere in Boston had his ambition run in the direction of a prosperous legal practice. George Otis Shattuck was to be Holmes's principal mentor in the office, though he gained much from his association with Peleg Chandler and James Bradley Thayer, who was later to be Royall Professor of Law at Harvard. Shattuck was not especially sympathetic to the speculative strain in the apprentice lawyer, nor did he offer encouragement to his philosophical predilections. Rather he taught Holmes that the lawyer's most important talent was that "of dealing with the actualities of daily life."[15] Shattuck, in short, helped to shape Holmes's eventual conviction that experience and not theory was the stuff of which the law was made. Holmes came to this awareness not because Shattuck preached it, but because he practiced it, with the fledgling lawyer suitably positioned at his elbow to watch the processes of law in the making. Though he may have missed the casebook method in Law School, he very early got a taste of the real thing from Shattuck.

Under the influence of Shattuck by day, Holmes, by night and by choice, became more deeply involved in the philosophical speculations of William James, Charles Peirce, Chauncey Wright, Nicholas St. J. Green, Joseph Warner, and John Chipman Gray—fellow members of the Metaphysical Club. The club, whose name was completely ironic, was an informal group of young intellectuals searching for answers to age-old questions by following the paths of science. Though he had cast his lot with the law, Wendell Holmes remained uncertain just how he might fuse his speculative preferences with legal training. In some respects, during these early years of legal experience, it still appeared to him that it might have to be an "either or" matter, that one must either practice law—and Boston offered prospects for success in such an endeavor for one of Holmes's background and ability—or one must throw it over in favor of an ivory tower. Nor was he alone in facing this dilemma. William James eventually struck out in the direction of medicine, without divorcing himself from philosophy, to become world renowned. But Charles Peirce remained wedded more exclusively to a search for ultimate meanings, while convinced there were none, and ended his days a forgotten giant.

During the period 1869–1873, Holmes began to appreciate the likelihood of merging his own predilections. In that time he commenced his work on the twelfth edition of *Kent's Commentaries,* published in 1873. He was also, from 1870 to 1873, coeditor of the *American Law Review,* a post in which he realized not a few opportunities, in book notices and editorial comments, to apply his scholarship (in which history was preferred to theory) to contemporary writings and issues. His purpose, explicit enough, was to contribute to advancing and changing the profession's understanding of law and of the growth of legal systems. In addition, Holmes served as a law lecturer at Harvard from 1870 to 1873, while engaging in practice with his younger brother, Edward. And he married Fanny Dixwell in 1872. These years were pregnant with meaning for the future public and private life of Oliver Wendell Holmes, Jr.

V *Metaphysical Club*

Allusions to Holmes's participation in the philosophical conversations of the Metaphysical Club are frequently made with the intention of suggesting what he derived from his association with this celebrated body. An equally pertinent consideration may well be what Holmes brought to these informal but highly charged discussions which profoundly affected the lives and careers of those involved after they went their separate ways. In this regard his Civil War experiences had been a unique preparation, foreshadowing his thesis of truth as that which one "can't help" but believe. Furthermore he was certainly thinking along scientific lines when he wrote William James in April of 1868 that "law as well as any other series of facts in the world may be approached in the interests of science."[16] Holmes "was led by his commitment to the scientific method to consider law as a series of facts not unlike those other series of facts with which the natural scientist is concerned. So looking upon the law, he came to believe that the series of facts known as law was susceptible to scientific consideration."[17] Such a conception of the law would become central to Holmes's efforts as scholar, jurist, justice, the experience of each phase of his life of the law confirming the feasibility of the scientific rule. By convincingly demonstrating that law no less than history, medicine, or logic was susceptible to scientific imperatives, Holmes provided the Metaphysical Club with one important supportive argument for an all-embracing empiricism.

At the same time Holmes took something from the dialogues of the Metaphysical Club which was vital to his life's enterprise. During the Civil War he faced the stark need to disregard the differentiation between the "ought" and "is." War taught him, as few other mentors might, that disasters are random, that fate is indiscriminate, that the good often die young. In this respect the Civil War had a permanent effect on him. When it came to the discussions of "is" and "ought" or of "good" and "bad" with his intellectual brotherhood, Chauncey Wright, a philosopher of the scientific spirit, above all others, persuaded him of the necessity of ignoring the "ought" on purely scientific grounds.[18] Something like this lesson Holmes learned in one of his first courtroom encounters. He was acting as junior counsel to Shattuck, as the firm represented a widow who was suing for a monetary judgment against the New York Central Railroad. It was the classic pattern of a lonely lady battling the giant corporation. The "is" and the "ought" were clearly delineated in the eye of the sentimentalist if not the moralist. But the case was decided in favor of the corporation on the basis of the law involved. Both Chauncey Wright's contentions and Shattuck's "dealings with the actualities of daily life" showed that nothing less than a scientific indifference to "right" and "wrong" would serve.

The give and take of the Metaphysical Club may well have contributed to another of Wendell Holmes's mature philosophical legal principles. His predictive theory of law, that the law is what the judges say it is, has been traced to the years when the influence of Wright, Peirce, and Nicholas St. J. Green, a Harvard Law School lecturer, was the most pronounced. It has been pointed out that in criticizing Austin's *Principles of Jurisprudence* in the *American Law Review* in 1870 he went no further than to say that the merit of the common law is that it decides the case first and determines the principle afterward. By 1872, however, he had moved visibly in the direction of his predictive theory when he wrote:

The only question for the lawyer is, how will the judges act? Any motive for their action, be it constitution, statute, custom, or precedent, which can be relied upon as likely in the generality of cases to prevail, is worthy of consideration as one of the sources of the law in a treatise on jurisprudence.[19]

Years later Holmes chose to put the dictum positively: "The prophecies of what the court will do in fact and nothing more pretentious, are what I mean by the law."[20] The origins of the predictive theory, viewed in this light, are hardly problematical.[21]

VI   Kent's Commentaries

In editing *Kent's Commentaries*, Holmes began his work as part of a two-man team but emerged as solely responsible for the completed task. James Kent, grandson of Chancellor Kent, initially invited James Bradley Thayer, one of Holmes's law lecturers at Harvard, to be the editor of what was planned as the twelfth edition of the *Commentaries*. Thayer, in turn, solicited help from the younger Holmes, and was so impressed by Holmes's preliminary annotations that he welcomed him as co-editor. Thayer had two reasons for doing this. James Kent wanted the edition to be completed in two years' time, manifestly impossible for an editor working alone to accomplish. Second, Thayer did not see fit to sacrifice so large a portion of his time from his thriving practice. Holmes, in contrast, viewed the whole enterprise as relieving him of the need to become drawn too deeply into litigation. The difficulties involved in coediting, as in coauthoring, are plain enough: in any such arrangement, if one of the individuals has both a more refined

taste and a greater thirst for the work at hand, while his partner
admits to the value of the enterprise but finds it disagreeable
nonetheless, the stage is set for imbalance. Holmes, eager to test
his scholarly worth, accepted that challenge. For nearly four
years *Kent's Commentaries* consumed him. After a while he
would go nowhere, not even to the dinner table, without his
green bag, the manuscript inside. His friends fretted about his
health; his look was wan and melancholy.[22]

The work involved in editing was no mere legal exercise.
Holmes cited every relevant case and statute which had been
handed down since the previous edition, to be sure; but he was
also concerned with putting such items into the kind of order
which typified the scientific spirit of the day. His aim was to
make the twelfth edition more useful by making it more usable.
On occasion, Holmes found opportunities to interpolate at least
some of the new anthropological and historical learning, thereby
bringing fresh understanding of the origins and growth of law.
Thus he began the task, a long and a fruitful one as it turned
out, of bringing his mind to bear on the meaning of law in
America and on what other legal scholars would come to understand by law. The "Holmesian" view of the legal universe had
taken an important step forward.

VII Scholar/Editor

Kent's *Commentaries* had plunged Holmes deep into the sea
of legal details. In contrast his contributions to the *American
Law Review*, beginning in 1867, enabled him better to relate to
the broad curve of the legal shore line, to measure currents, to
assess new intellectual tides which were reshaping the law.
The *Commentaries* were history past; his pieces for the *American Law Review* were law in the making. From 1870 to 1873
Holmes served with Arthur G. Sedgwick as coeditor of the
Review, having given valuable assistance to the previous editors, John Chipman Gray and John C. Ropes, in the years before.
Holmes, in fact, had done as many as a dozen reviews for the
journal before coming on as coeditor, including a long commentary dealing with the impeachment proceedings against President Johnson.[23] Several examples of Holmes's work deserve

attention because of the light they shed on his increasingly empirical view of the law. In his own phrase, "the law is not a science, but is essentially empirical."[24] In various book notices he quoted Savigny approvingly that "customs may repeal statute,"[25] and applauded American neglect of Roman Civil Law, not on a basis of theory but of practicality.[26] His review of Roscoe's *Digest of the Law Evidence in Criminal Cases* praised the *Digest* because the structure employed was "not unlike that which is pursued in treatises on Natural History, and which has been followed with advantage in some psychological works." Holmes complimented Roscoe because he had brought together a useful digest without seeking to demonstrate a theory.[27] His criticism furthermore reflected the general influence of John Stuart Mill as well as the more particular impact of having read Fitzjames Stephen, who in his *General View of the Criminal Law of England,* advanced the proposition that "the ultimate reason for believing is that without belief men can not act."[28] This strain of British empiricism Holmes would digest fully, of course, yet he was to refine it to suit his own needs. But most importantly, in these years he was fusing law and philosophy in such a way as to both motivate and explain his mature assertions.

The young editor's ability to keep politics disentangled from law was well illustrated when in the columns of the *American Law Review* he addressed himself to the various issues raised by Reconstruction: the impeachment of Andrew Johnson, the constitutionality of the Force Bill, the nature of sovereignty in the American federal union. In the case of Johnson's impeachment, Holmes expressed his judgment that the president's best defense would be founded on the statutes involved rather than in the murky waters of constitutional meaning. Closely related to the presidential impeachment was the question of the enforceability of the Reconstruction Acts, should the Supreme Court declare them unconstitutional. Once again Holmes refused to be led by theory—that a law declared null and void by the Court was a law eternally condemned—preferring to look at the facts of a specific situation in formulating "a principle of public policy."[29] Such conclusions pointed, almost inevitably, to a consideration of the nature and locus of sovereignty. In after

years, as he observed to Harold Laski, the sovereignty of the
state "asserts itself as omnipotent in the sense that what it sees
fit to order, it will make you obey."[30] But the Holmes of the
American Law Review no less than the Holmes of the Supreme
Court emphasized that sovereignty rested not on a theory of
the state but on the realities of the moment.

In his capacity as *Law Review* editor Holmes also insisted,
as he did in other situations and at later times, on rejecting the
"ought" in the application of the law. Comments on the Gas-
Stokers case in 1873 registered this view. His willingness to
discuss the case, which had to do with the workmen in England
who had gone on strike and who were jailed for conspiring to
break a contract, also underscored his growing awareness of the
reciprocity of legal ideas between England and America. He
based his position on what he thought of as the facts at hand,
condemning the imprisonment of the workers, but not on the
grounds of injustice or inhumanity or immorality. Such considerations were not relevant to the law. In the evolution of an
industrial society the strength of labor, realistically considered,
had reached the point where it was dangerous if not suicidal to
cast recalcitrant workers into prison. Neither a theory of law
nor a set of philosophical absolutes had anything to do with it.
"If the welfare of the living majority is paramount it can only
be on the ground that the majority have power in their hands.
The fact is that legislation . . . is empirical. It is necessarily made
a means by which a body, having power, puts burdens which
are disagreeable to them, on the shoulders of some body else."[31]
What was germane was the power which workers had acquired
and which Darwinism made intelligible for any one who was
willing to look at the facts.

The appointment of Oliver Wendell Holmes, Jr., as Lecturer
in Law at Harvard in 1870—he would lecture on constitutional
law and jurisprudence—was both recognition of the competence
of the serious young legal thinker and an opportunity for his
further reflections on those aspects of the law which were especially attractive to him at the time. Of the two, recognition
and opportunity, the latter proved to be the more valuable. All
during the decade of the 1870s, Holmes, by dint of his relentless
application to the study of law, was maturing ideas which would

eventuate in publication of *The Common Law*. Some ten years
and more before the appearance of that memorable book in
1881 he was responding to the findings of other legal authorities
and engaged in creatively examining his own perceptions. For
example, he was persuaded, to a degree, at least, of the need
to make legal classifications based on duties rather than rights,
as he read Austin and James Bryce. But he was prepared to reject
the one-dimensional conception of sovereignty which the
English scholar Austin had assimilated from his intensive study
of Roman law. At least in the American republic, Holmes argued,
sovereignty was many sided. Public opinion, for example, might
weaken or strengthen the exercise of what was termed the
"sovereign will." In a word, the early years of the decade of the
1870s were seminal. What Holmes was aiming at was the living
element in law, what made law alive at a given time in history.
Law was something larger than the command of the sovereign,
because various factors went into causing the command of the
sovereign to be obeyed. This "living" quality was a variant of the
empirical, the specific, the unique, and thus did not lend itself
to easy classification. Indeed, classification could be deadly, because it tended to drive out the living elements and to substi-
tute for them some theory or other. It was in response to Austin,
as has been shown, that Holmes offered the first identifiable
intimation of his predictive theory of law.

The creative juices had begun to flow in Holmes. He had so
far thought or written but a fraction of what he eventually
would contribute to legal knowledge. But he had gained an all-
important confidence in himself as an original thinker. In the
long view it mattered little that his contemporaries were arriving
at his conclusions independent of him, for after all he was
coming to these same conclusions independent of them. He was
in the midst of discovering the feasibility of merging law and
philosophy. It was to be a novel philosophy, radical in com-
parison, empirical in basis, and pragmatic in thrust, making the
outlines of the historical Holmes distinct and discernible.

CHAPTER 3

Holmes and The Common Law

I *The Private Man*

WITH publication of *Kent's Commentaries* Holmes's private life temporarily, and uncharacteristically, overshadowed his scholarly preoccupation. Marriage had ordained it, though the event was delayed in coming. In May of 1874, Mr. and Mrs. Oliver Wendell Holmes, Jr., set sail for England and a much-deserved respite from the toil which they had shared. Upon their return in the autumn, plans were made to move from the household of Dr. Holmes, where they had lived since their wedding, to their own quarters. This parting, if bittersweet, nonetheless marked a major change in Holmes's private affairs. Though the reasons for living with the Auotcrat were practical, that is, a real want of income, few married men wait until their thirty-third year to leave the nest. It is no exaggeration to say that the son breathed a sigh of relief upon his formal exit from his father's house. This event in a long-postponed coming of age was premised on a prior development, the formation in May of 1873 of a partnership with George Otis Shattuck and William A. Munroe. Holmes was, in consequence, a full-fledged practitioner of the law. While Shattuck, the most senior of the partners, did not expect him to bring in many clients, he was confident that the firm would be successful enough.[1] Fanny and Wendell Holmes were happy to live modestly in their flat above a Beacon Street drugstore, once they could live with and for themselves alone. Only the law would be a welcome intruder in their midst. That the law would indeed intrude neither of them doubted—or feared. By joining with Shattuck and Munroe Holmes had not changed his spots. Practice by day, scholarship by night, commencing with the

51

autumn of 1874, was to be the regimen out of which grew his great book, *The Common Law*. Luckily for Holmes, who had something of an obsession about achieving a major success before he reached the age of forty, the book was published early in March 1881.[2]

The London phase of the 1874 summer abroad lived up to Holmes's considerable expectations. He visited once again with any number of British acquaintances. At the Alpine Club he made a new friend in Frederick E. Pollock, whose father, Sir Frederick, was Queen's Remembrancer. Holmes already knew of the younger Pollock, a budding legal scholar himself, by reason of his paper "Law and Command." Soon after this first meeting they launched their famous correspondence. London was again as impressed with Holmes as he was with London. "You have to pay your way in London. No one takes you on faith—and I love it," he later was to recall,[3] an awareness and an appreciation which London's intelligentsia warmly reciprocated.[4]

The pattern of Holmes's 1874 visit was remarkably similar to his 1866 sojourn. He and his wife "toured" the Continent, their itinerary taking them as far south as Venice, with stops in Paris and Geneva along the way. By August they were happy to be back in England once more in the company of distinguished hosts. Holmes talked long and seriously with some of the reigning intellects of the law, the brothers Stephen, Sir Henry Maine, Lord James Bryce, and Sir George Otto Trevelyan among them. He was able to discern that his already well-formed if still embryonic conception of the law as that which the courts would enforce was well received in law circles in Britain. And he had gotten in an altogether personal and private way the kind of recognition which, as has been suggested before, was vital to his further efforts. It was the younger Pollock who remarked, "I thoroughly agree that the only definition of law for a lawyer's purpose is something which the Court will enforce," adding further that "the true theory is that all attempts to get a scientific measure are out of place and we can only seek a rough measure in the average opinion of the community—or such of the community as are accustomed to dealings of the kind in question."[5] The fact that Englishmen like Pollock and the magis-

terial Frederick W. Maitland applauded his work more en-
thusiastically than his American colleagues helped to make the
summer of 1874 memorable and meaningful.

Back at home, the routine nature of the legal work of Shattuck,
Holmes, and Munroe should not disguise the influence of the
"daily practicalities of the law" on Wendell Holmes. If the
firm was engaged in conventional legal matters, so much the
better for an appreciation of law as it was made in and by
the courts. Holmes's predictive theory was being reenforced by
his own examination of law in process. For Holmes the historian,
this was instructive, watching law being developed at the
grass roots, the vivid understanding of which he carried back
to his nocturnal researches. As an advocate before the bench
Holmes might well have thought of himself as a contributor—
as countless men of the law across the centuries had been contributors—to legal formation, attempting always to blend history and principle.[6] Yet often enough he encountered in-
consistencies between theory and practice which to his scholar's
eye only demonstrated the sheer complexity of legal evolution.
In more than one court case he discovered the judges handing
down decisions on the basis of precedent, the originating conditions of which had vanished long since. As a student of law,
he was far less alarmed by the potential injustice of this procedure than he was provoked to examine the history of the
common law. His purpose was to show that legislation was not
the product of sovereign authority but of social customs, essentially instable, which were cast in the form of statutes to be
used for a while. Holmes's steadily expanding knowledge as a
counselor at law confirmed his assertion, uttered in the opening sentences of *The Common Law,* that the life of the law
was not logic but experience.

II *Contours of Legal Thought*

In the 1870s American legal thought—jurisprudence—was
ripe for change, and a number of young American scholars
besides Holmes—men like Melville Bigelow, James Bradley
Thayer, and James Barr Ames—were aware of it. Along with
Holmes they would contribute to making certain fundamental

alterations in the legal framework. From the time of Jeremy Bentham political commentators had called for a reworking of the legal system in order to make it more intelligible and more practical. Nor were these demands for reform confined to England. German scholars especially, and Savigny above all others, had been delving deeply into legal history since the early years of the nineteenth century. Their views of the law were based on new research into ancient legal forms. An interest in Roman law, wherein the sovereign authority seemed clearly to promulgate the rules according to which society was regulated, dovetailed nicely with fresh developments in German philosophy. The categorical imperative of Kant and the inexorable dialectic of Hegel were called upon by legal scholars to provide a contemporary philosophical rationale to an ancient system of law, recast for use by a modern generation. The result of all this was to introduce metaphysical concepts of absolute right and absolute prohibition, flowing chiefly from Kant's principal contentions that man is an end in himself and that his rights and duties can not be reduced to social convenience. This kind of argument Holmes totally opposed. A Malthusian and a social Darwinist, he saw in the cruelty and the struggle for life its basic reality. If law was to be evaluated properly, it must be according to empirical criteria, however much this might offend morality or sentiment. All of Holmes's efforts as a legal authority would come under the influence of such hard certainties, and he sought to persuade others of the cogency of his position by his writings throughout the 1870s. His long article "Primitive Notions in Modern Law," which appeared in the *American Law Review* in April of 1876 and which foreshadowed his discussion of liability in *The Common Law*, for example, grew out of his investigations and analysis of what history revealed concerning the nature and source of law.

Philosophical considerations must be read in conjunction with certain trends in American jurisprudence. In the aftermath of the Revolution, American common-law rules were more and more frequently challenged. The common law was no longer conceived as a body of fixed doctrine which judges applied to factual situations. As one authority explains, "by

1820 the process of common law decision-making had taken on many of the qualities of legislation. As judges began to conceive of common law adjudication as a process of making and not merely discovering legal rules, they were led to form general doctrine based on a self-conscious consideration of social and economic policies."[7] This drastic alteration in the role of the common law manifested itself, for example, in the rule that a person could not be convicted of a federal crime without a federal statute. In the larger setting such a ruling was needed to prevent the national government from so extending its authority as to obliterate the jurisdiction of the states. Equally significant was the changing view of the law as a social and economic instrument, an adjustment occasioned by the vast differences between conditions in old England which had given rise to common law rules and those of an expanding American nation which faced new and unique problems associated with multi-dimensional growth. In this developing instrumentalism, it was a case of the "ascendency of substance over form." But by mid-century these new modes of the law had themselves hardened into a set of formal legal rules. The advantages obtained by the rising economic power-groups could best be retained through alliance with and reliance on the legal profession. For its part the profession had to struggle to master a law which was more and more complex, demanding a more analytical and thus a more professional approach. Lawyers treated the law as scientific, objective, and apolitical. The resultant combination of "power and intellect" added up to legal formalism, with which Holmes was to do battle almost as soon as he began to think and act as a man of the law.

In addition to philosophical and jurisprudential trends, there were other specific influences at work on Holmes's mind, directly and immediately. In 1876 Henry Adams published *Essays in Anglo-Saxon Law,* in which he and his fellow contributors argued forcefully that the roots and the strength of Anglo-American legal institutions derived from Teutonic rather than from Roman origins. The inferences flowing from this contention were of the utmost consequence for Holmes. It meant that law did not have its provenance in the will of the emperor or the laws of the Senate, with decree and statute, aided by acceptance and usage, rendered immutable. Instead, a search for the sources of Anglo-American law led back to the customs of Teutonic or Frankish tribes, customs which were susceptible to slow but sure alteration, and thus were not in nature fixed or final. This conviction regarding the origins of Anglo-American law "formed perhaps the most important foundation stone of Holmes's writing in the second half of the 1870s and therefore of *The Common Law*."[8]

Such an assumption can be identified in all five essays which Holmes did for the *American Law Review* between 1876 and 1880. That these essays won for their author a solid reputation in Boston/Cambridge legal circles is reason sufficient to explain the invitation which Holmes received to deliver the Lowell Lectures for 1880. This series consisted of twelve individual lectures given at Huntington Hall in Tremont Street in November and December of that year. In turn these lectures, refined and expanded and supplemented by additional treatments of criminal law and contracts, became *The Common Law*.[9]

III The Common Law *Examined*

A. Prolegomenon

In the opening sentence of the great book Holmes spoke his objective: "to present a general view of the Common Law." He proposed a methodology: "We must alternately consult history and existing theories of legislation." And finally he stated his purpose: to understand the law, for which today "there are a great many rules which are quite sufficiently accounted for by their manifest good sense, . . . there are some which can only be understood by reference to the infancy of procedure among the German tribes, or to the social condition of Rome under the Decemvirs."[10] In laying down these general propositions Holmes offered two caveats. "One, is that of supposing because an idea seems very familiar and natural to us, that it has always been so." The other is "the opposite of asking too much of history. We start with the man full grown. It may be assumed that the earliest barbarians whose practices are to be considered, had a good many of the feelings and passions as ourselves"(6). Asking his listeners—and later his readers—to bear in mind such principles,

Holmes proceeded to expound the common law with boldness and originality.

B. Liability

He first construed the early forms of liability, holding that "early English appeals for personal violence," for example, "seem to have been confined to intentional wrongs" (7). "Intentional" character implied moral culpability, to be sure. But could an inanimate thing, a falling tree, a runaway wagon, in any way be considered morally responsible for injuries sustained in an accident? For that matter, could the ferocious dog be held responsible for biting his owner's neighbor? Moral culpability must be confined to moral agents. Yet early law took vengeance upon the offending object: the fallen tree whose chips were scattered to the wind. As civilization advanced, vengeance was replaced by compensation, and liability was transferred from the agent to the responsible owner. As Holmes pointed out, "the customs, beliefs, or needs of a primitive time establish a rule or a formula. In the course of centuries the custom, belief, or necessity disappears, but the rules remain. The reason which gave rise to the rule has been forgotten, and ingenious minds set themselves to inquire how it is to be accounted for. Some ground of policy is thought of, which seems to explain it and reconcile it with the present state of things; and then the rule adapts itself to the new reasons which have been found for it, and enters on a new career"(8). As an example, Holmes suggested that in Roman legal procedures the desire for revenge applied initially to torts, a practice which sooner or later was applied to a breach of contract, because "the remedies for the two are not found ready made"(14). Furthermore, Holmes argued for similarities between Roman law and German tribal custom; that is, vengeance developed imperceptibly toward a nonviolent satisfaction for the injury committed, while moral culpability replaced the animism ascribed to ships, wagons, and mad dogs.

Conclusions drawn from such considerations enabled Holmes to reject the conservative understanding of law as something fixed and final. Looked at logically, "each new decision follows syllogistically from existing precedent. . . . Precedents survive

in the law long after the use they once served is at an end and the
reason for them forgotten. The result of following them must
often be failure and confusion from the merely logical point of
view"(31). So much for form. But what about the substance of
law? Law is made by judges on "considerations of what is expedi-
ent for the community concerned. Every important principle
which is developed by litigation is in fact and at bottom the result of more or less definitely understood views of public policy;
most generally, to be sure, under our practice and traditions, the
unconscious result of the instinctive preferences and inarticulate
convictions, but none the less traceable to views of public policy
in the last analysis"(32). Law, in Holmes's own words, was administered by able and experienced men who know too much to
sacrifice good sense to the syllogism (32). This explication of early
forms of liability concluded on two notable observations. One,
the law "is forever adopting new principles from life at one end,
and it always retains old ones from history at the other, which
have not yet been absorbed or sloughed off"(32). In so saying,
Holmes was stating a basically pragmatic principle as applied to
the law. Two, "while the law does still and always, in a certain
sense, measure legal liability by moral standards, it nevertheless,
by the very necessity of its nature, is continually transmuting
those moral standards into external or objective ones from which
the actual guilt of the party concerned is wholly eliminated."
This latter axiom he then set about to demonstrate by an examination of criminal law(33).

C. Criminal Law

Holmes commenced his treatment of criminal law by contending that presentment was "the child of vengeance," and this
desire "imparts an opinion that its object is actually and personally to blame"(34–35).[11] But the question is whether such a
standard is still appropriate in contemporary society. While admitting that any form of punishment satisfied a thirst for vengeance in some way, and that criminal law had improved only
gradually, still the modern view of criminal law, Holmes thought,
must be punishment meted out to protect society from actions
harmful to it and to its members. Punishment is not intended to

reform the criminal but to deter crime. If the prisoner pays with his body, society benefits. This social reference is crucial, of course, to Holmes's understanding of all law. In criminal matters as well as in others, "the first requirement of a sound body of law is that it should correspond with the actual feelings and demands of the community, whether right or wrong"(36). Holmes believed that the law should not encourage the passion of revenge, either in individuals or the state.

The social aspect of criminal law was brought out in still another way. Taking direct issue with the Kantian proposition that the individual can never be sacrificed, can never be treated as a means to an end, Holmes asserted, "Probably most English-speaking lawyers would accept the preventive theory without much hesitation. No society has ever admitted that it could not sacrifice individual welfare to its own existence, as both military conscription and the right of eminent domain demonstrate"(37). Such a contention led Holmes to utter one of his most famous dicta: "The *ultimata ratio,* not only *regnum,* but of private persons, is force, and . . . at the bottom of all private relations however tempered by sympathy and all the social feelings, is justified self-preference"(38). Thus Holmes was urging that the general principles of criminal and civil liability were the same. If the criminal were judged morally, not socially, his abnormal instincts, his want of education, his lack of intelligence, and whatever other defects he might exhibit would have to be taken into account. Yet for the most part these matters were subordinate to what was thought best by society for society as specified in laws and judicial opinions. The individual, therefore, was a means, "a tool to increase the general welfare at his own expense"(40). Such a position, Holmes was to admit, was not an all-encompassing rule. For example, the principle of killing in self-defense is sanctioned by society—and in the interest of society—even though the act of killing is indeed intentional. On the other hand, ignorance of the law can never be allowed to excuse its violation. Society would surely be the loser if it permitted violation of the law because the offender could plead ignorance. The social fabric would disintegrate, and society would be doomed. Without intending to deny the possible importance of "personal unworthiness," the purpose of criminal law was "to induce external conformity to rule." Even so, personal blameworthiness "was judged according to standards set by society"(43). This was exemplified in Holmes's argument that "according to current morality, a man is not so much to blame for an act done under the disturbance of great excitement, caused by a wrong done to himself, as when he is calm"(51). The matter of house-burning was another set piece employed by Holmes to illustrate his views. A man may intentionally destroy his own property. But if his house is in close proximity to others and these houses are fired in consequence, he is guilty of arson in as much as the effect of his action has had evil social results. Holmes neatly summarized his theory of criminal liability as follows: "All acts are indifferent *per se*. Acts are rendered criminal because they are done under circumstances in which they will probably cause some harm which the law seeks to prevent. The test of criminality in such cases is the degree of danger shown by such experience to attend that act under those circumstances" (61). In this step-by-step way, he elucidated and established the social character of criminal activity.

D. Torts

Having delineated the social origins of law in matters relating to civil liability and crime, Holmes proceeded to apply the same yardstick to torts. The business of the law of torts, as he stated it in *The Common Law*, "is to fix the dividing line between those cases in which a man is liable for harm he has done, and those in which he is not" (64).[12] If the law requires satisfaction, "the reason for doing so must be found in some general view of conduct which every one may fairly expect and demand from every other, whether that other has agreed to it or not" (63). The law of torts admittedly abounds in moral phraseology—malice, fraud, intent, and negligence—all of which implies that a guilty person must have had some moral shortcoming (30). While certain authorities, like Austin, accepted such a conclusion, others insisted that man always acted at his own peril. Holmes proposed to advance an alternate theory, namely, that man acted at his own peril insofar as society would expect a prudent man to act and to foresee the consequences of his actions. And inasmuch as the expectations of society change, the law itself may change accordingly. Such modifications in the expectations of society were always "politic"—that is, according to public policy, or what the public would support. As Holmes wrote, "a man may have as bad a heart as he chooses, if his conduct is within the rules" (88). The standards of the law were external standards. Law was wholly indifferent to the internal phenomenon of conscience. It was in his discussion of torts that Holmes offered one of his most incisive descriptions of the life of the law:

The growth of the law is very apt to take place in this way. Two widely different cases suggest a general distinction, which is a clear one when stated broadly. But as new cases cluster around the opposite poles, and begin to approach each other, the distinction becomes more difficult to trace; the determinations are made one way or the other on a very slight preponderance of feeling, rather than of articulate reason; and at last a mathematical line is arrived at by the contact of contrary decisions, which is so far arbitrary that it might equally well have been drawn a little farther to the one side or the other, but which must have been drawn somewhere in the neighborhood of where it falls.

In this way exact distinctions have been worked out upon questions in which the elements to be considered are few. For instance, what is a reasonable time for presenting negotiable paper, or what is a difference in kind and what a difference only in quality, or the rule against perpetuities. (101)

Just as law grew in response to the needs of society, so social requirements took precedence over those of the individual. The law "does not attempt to see men as God sees them." It only considers what is blameworthy in the average man, a determination made by society and not by moral theories.

The "actual wickedness of the kind described" in the use of such words as fraud or malice "is not an element in the civil wrongs to which those words are applied," thought Holmes (104). The basis of liability in torts was the knowledge of what effect the actions performed would have. One example, fraud, may suffice to illustrate Holmes's viewpoint. Deceit was a necessary element in fraud, and as such a "notion drawn from the moral world, and in its popular sense distinctly imports wickedness." The "elements which make it immoral are the knowledge that the statement is false, and the intention that it shall be acted upon" (106). But the defendant in an action involving fraud is chargeable not because he committed an immoral act but because of proof that he knew the other party intended to act upon deceitful information. "The standard of what is called intention is thus really an external standard" of known circumstances (107). Looked at critically, "we find the moral side shade away" (108). Notwithstanding such bold assertions of the social cast of the law, Holmes was prompted to state "the moral starting-point of liability in general should never be forgotten, and the law can not without disregarding it hold a man answerable for statements based on facts which would have convinced a wise and prudent man of their truth" (109). Such a concession to morality was indeed a qualified one, for Holmes went on to observe that "starting from the moral ground [the common law] works out an external standard of what would be fraudulent in the average prudent member of the community, and requires every member at his peril to avoid that" (109). In such a context Holmes was led to make one of his most succinct explanations about the growth of law:

The theory of torts may be summed up very simply. At the two extremes of the law are rules determined by policy without references of any kind to morality. Certain harms a man may inflict even wickedly; for certain others he must answer, although his conduct has been prudent and beneficial to the community.

But in the main the law started from those intentional wrongs which are the simplest and most pronounced cases, as well as the nearest to the feeling of revenge which leads to self-redress. It thus naturally adopted the vocabulary and in some degree the tests, of morals. But as the law has grown even when its standards have continued to model themselves upon those of morality, they have necessarily become external, because they have considered, not the actual condition of the particular defendant, but whether his conduct would have been wrong in the fair average member of the community, whom he is expected to equal at his peril. (128)

For Holmes the socially external standard must always be the determining standard.

E. Bailments

This critical approach to the law Holmes illustrated in his treatment of bailment. Admitting that the only existing theories on the subject came from Germany and that "the German philosophers who have written upon the law have known no other system than Roman," some rules which he discovered in his research, lay clearly against what the German legal theorists had come to regard as first principles (133). At least Holmes wanted to avoid the hasty assumption that such principles were universal; in fact, he had discovered procedures which were kindred to early German folk-laws. While not claiming that the law of bailment was of pure German descent, Holmes argued that it possessed enough German elements to challenge the German philosophers who had insisted on Roman sources. Occasionally in *The Common Law*, the author was satisfied to question existing assumptions without offering a new thesis fully limned (130–139).

F. Possession

Holmes took a critical attitude in discussing "possession." He again came out openly and unequivocally against the "*a priori* doctrines of Kant and Hegel," as well as those of "the speculative jurists of Germany, from Savigny to Ihering" (163). Disagreement arose from the German claim to universal authority. To Holmes the "possessing of a right as such was intrinsically absurd" (265). Tracing theories from Kant back to Rousseau and the Massachusetts version of the American Bill of Rights, he dismissed them one and all inasmuch as they made man an end unto himself. Thus, if an individual was in possession of a thing, the law protected him in that possession because it was an extension of the self. Absolutism of this sort was anathema to Holmes. He was "one who saw in the history of law the development of society" and who was "apt to think that the proximate ground of law must be empirical" (168). "Law being a practical thing must found itself on actual forces." (168). Possession was to Holmes a matter of instinct which he was prepared to argue forcefully.

It is quite enough, therefore, for the law, that man, by an instinct which he shares with the domestic dog, and of which the seal gives a most striking example, will not allow himself to be dispossessed, either by force or fraud, of what he holds, without trying to get it back again. Philosophy may find a hundred reasons to justify the instinct, but it would be totally immaterial if it should condemn it and bid us surrender without a murmur. As long as the instinct remains, it will be more comfortable for the law to satisfy it in an orderly manner, than to leave people to themselves. If it should do otherwise, it would become a matter for pedagogues, wholly devoid of reality. (168)

In short, instinct was "that mightier body of law than the Roman" (166).

Because Holmes was writing about "possession" at a time when property rights had taken on a sacred patina in American society, he was moved to discuss the nature of "rights" at some length in his chapter on Possession. It may be particularly useful to quote him fully, for by inference he was evaluating all rights, not excluding the "inalienable rights" of life, liberty, and the pursuit of happiness as expressed in the American tradition.

A legal right is nothing but a permission to exercise certain natural powers, and upon certain conditions to obtain protection, restitution, or compensation by the aid of the public force. Just so far as the aid of the public force is given a man, he has a legal right, and this right is the same whether his claim is founded on righteousness or iniquity. Just so far as possession is protected, it is as much a source of legal rights as ownership is when it secures the same protection.

Every right is a consequence attached by the law to one or more facts which the law defines, and wherever the law gives any one special rights not shared by the body of the people, it does so on the ground that special facts, not true of the rest of the world, are true of him. When a group of facts thus singled out by the law exists in the case of a given person, he is said to be entitled to the corresponding rights; meaning thereby, that the law helps him to constrain his neighbors, or some of them, in a way in which it would not, if all the facts in question were not true of him. (169)

Such considerations were of course legal. "What may be their relation to moral rights if there are any, and whether moral rights are not in like manner logically the off-spring of moral duties, are questions which do not concern us" (173). Such concern was for the speculative philosopher who approached the law from outside, while the jurist came to his subject from within.

G. Contracts

In his analysis of the law, Holmes was imparting objectivity by reference to the rules of society and public policy. This he carried over to his discussion of contracts, one of the most sensitive and historic of all legal considerations. The common element in all contracts is a promise. One promise may be distinguished from another—for example, I promise you 100 bales of cotton—by the degree of power possessed by the promisor over the event involved. But according to Holmes, the law does not require the promisor to have any assurance that he either can or will deliver on the promise made. In the moral world it may be an obligation to promise only what one can fulfill, but not so at law. "I take it that a man may bind himself at law that any future event shall happen" (234).[12] By so arguing, Holmes escaped the idea that a contract was a "qualified subjection of one will to another, a kind of limited slavery" (235). Equally practical for contemporary social requirements, damages levied in a breach of contract were not as great as those justified in tort (236). Furthermore, when contracts were voided, the law displayed no concern with the actual state of the party's mind. "In contract, as elsewhere, [the law] must go by externals and judge parties by their conduct" (242). If there are distinctions which might account for voided contracts, these distinctions were "founded in experience, not in logic"—an observation which leads back unerringly to the prolegomena of *The Common Law* (244). Holmes had come full circle. Having commenced his investigation of the common law by noting that the "felt necessities" of the time were more critical to understanding the nature of law than was philosophy, he had but to reiterate this central proposition in order to conclude that the law-making process was a pragmatic exercise.

IV   The Common Law *Evaluated*

Contemporaries hailed *The Common Law,* Maitland for one contending that it would "leave its mark wide and deep on all the best thoughts of Americans and Englishmen about the history of their common law."[13] Latter day authorities have been no less extravagant in their praise of what has become a classic treatment in legal history. Yet Holmes's legal/historical exploration raises some issues, and occasions some questions. Obviously it is less than fair to fault him for his historical scholarship by the simple device of applying present-day standards.

Problems, nonetheless, remain. One of these is the narrowness of Holmes's frame of reference. This might be said to be characteristic of the Holmesian vision (or merely version) of life as well as of the law. It is notorious, for example, that Holmes, for all his admiration for Louis D. Brandeis—who later served with him on the Supreme Court of the United States—could not be persuaded by his friend to view in person the tenements and sweatshops which lay behind Brandeis's sociological briefs. This suggests a certain limitation in Holmes. May it not be argued as well that Holmes revealed definite lapses in his zeal to externalize the law, lapses traceable to the narrowness of his perspectives? Throughout his analysis in *The Common Law,* he insisted on social values as normative, while dismissing personal moral worthiness as largely irrelevant. But as a scholar who prided himself on eschewing metaphysics, that fact alone inhibited him from speculating on the how and the wherefore of these same social values. He was anxious to tell his audience that social values were mutable. But he did not take up any consideration of the source of such values which, in fact, are derived from individual private preferences. Taken in the aggregate, these become social values, moral in origin. Determined to delimit morality as an individual phenomenon in the law, Holmes overlooked social morality in its essence, while justifying or repudiating laws in social terms. Can Holmes be excused from his lapse because he was not interested in the source of social values? On his own terms, the answer must be "yes," since this was an area of inquiry which he chose not to pursue. But it must be borne in mind that Holmes was not talking about theory, but about the actuality of the law in daily affairs. Though he proposed to advance force as the *ultima ratio,* the society which was his constant reference point simply did not accept this dictum as a working principle, despite spot evidence that it did. To contend otherwise is to misread American history in the last years of the nineteenth century, as Holmes himself was aware when he wrote in the *Lochner* case that a large part of the country did not subscribe to Herbert Spencer's *Social Statics.* And to say that society ought to have embraced force, in light of all that Holmes had argued and social Darwinists were preaching, simply introduces an 'ought" factor which Holmes always had scorned. He seemed to say that the logic of history required society to dismiss traditional morality, whereas experience disclosed that it was otherwise. Holmes's failure to consult the human experience surrounding him in a matter so vital to his total intellectual position is ironic, to say the least. Ironies may indeed be an especially useful clue for assessing the Holmesian temperament, as the Holmesian temperament may be the master key for an appreciation of Holmes in history.

V *Professor of Law*

Temperament helps to explain Holmes's brief tenure as a professor of law at Harvard and his rapid advancement to the Supreme Judicial Court of Massachusetts.[14] Such human feelings as ambition, "justified self-interest," pride in accomplishment, and passion for recognition were all bound up in his choice of career. Certain negative attitudes, chief among them his active dislike of legal practice, must also figure in any evaluation. This latter consideration was prominent in Holmes's acceptance of the Harvard Law School appointment in January of 1882.

Despite submergence for many years in legal research on *The Common Law,* Oliver Wendell Holmes, Jr., was hardly an obscure figure in Boston/Cambridge circles when his book was published in 1881, and his prospects for further distinction, whether in academe or the judiciary, were exceptional. No later than the fall of 1881, talk was heard of Holmes being invited to join the Law School faculty. At any rate, on November 1 he wrote a letter to President Eliot indicating his readiness to accept an appointment and at the same time registering a number of provisos. The most important of these was to the effect that "if a judgeship should be offered me I should not wish to feel bound in honor not to consider it." This proposition had clearcut implications. Holmes's interest in a long-term academic career was considerably less than his desire to serve in the judiciary. On the other hand, a professorship of law seemed infinitely preferable to legal practice. The Law School would relieve him of the need to deal with clients and provide him with more time for scholarship. It might enhance his opportunities for fusing law and philosophy, though he was coming to have some reservations about the feasibility of that endeavor.[15] Holmes may even have been looking over his shoulder at his father, who had been a professor in the Medical School for many years.

Though he would not commence teaching until the fall, Holmes attended meetings of the Law School faculty in May and no doubt had a hand in his course assignments for September. This new position made it possible for him to visit abroad again with his wife. Some weeks in England seeing old friends— Bryce, Pollock, Leslie Stephen—were followed by Paris and journeying to a number of Swiss and German cities. According to habit the couple returned to spend time in England before the voyage home. And then the Law School became his domain. In his first Harvard lectures he easily and naturally advanced his historical research, adding to the impression that perhaps he was in his proper groove after all.

Yet within a short while—December of 1882—he had thrown up this career without hesitation when offered a state judgeship. Such a move is readily explained at the surface level of events, given his warning to President Eliot in the letter of November 1. But, down deeper, Holmes was responding to his own principle, proclaimed in *The Common Law*, of the "instinct for self-advancement," or as another New Englander of years before, Honest John Adams, had put it, "the passion for distinction." That practical sense which passed on to him from his Puritan forebears and perhaps more particularly from the Jackson side of the family would be better satisfied on the bench than in the lecture hall. As Holmes wrote to James Bryce, the British scholar-statesman, in December of 1882, "I did not think one could without moral loss decline any share in the practical struggle of life . . . and for which one believed himself fitter."[16] Beyond such considerations a judgeship would enable him to apply his philosophical generalizations to legal particulars: the fusing of philosophy and law was more the work of a sitting judge than a research scholar. He had said as much in *The Common Law* for any one who cared to read between the lines. His ambition to become a justice of the Supreme Court of Massachusetts can surprise no one who ponders his recurring argument that the law is what the judges say it is. To be a judge and make the law, this is the overriding and unifying reason why Wendell Holmes left Cambridge for Boston and the heat of battle and for which, temperamentally, he was the better suited.

VI   *The Author Precedes the Judge*

The varied activities of Holmes in the years from 1874 to 1882 should not obscure the central fact that he had come into his own as an author during this period and that he had written a momentous book. The depth of his research compared favorably with Gibbon; the sweep of his argument ranked with him Macaulay; the impact of his conclusions placed his work alongside that of Jefferson and Harriet Beecher Stowe as an author whose writings helped to change the course of American history. From the standpoint of the development of public institutions it would be difficult to class any book written in America before 1881 higher than *The Common Law*. At this stage of his career, though he hoped for more, Holmes was content to analyze and explain the history of Anglo-Saxon legal principles. This enterprise filled his days as it fulfilled his intellectual ambitions. Few writers ever have taken themselves more seriously. Holmes would not have required a judicial career to prove the worth of his ideas as presented in *The Common Law*, but having later attained recognition as an important public figure his work as a writer tends to be diminished. A book, rather than a career, was nonetheless at the center of the stage in the years from 1874 to 1882, a reminder of how the author preceded the judge in the unfolding of Holmes in history.[17]

CHAPTER 4

Scholar as Sitting Judge

I Sets of Convictions

OLIVER Wendell Holmes, Jr., assumed his place on the Massachusetts Supreme Judicial Court in January of 1883. He became the chief justice in 1899, remaining for virtually twenty years a ranking state jurist. During this period he worked unstintingly, applying many of the principles and hypotheses he had advanced in *The Common Law*.[1] The epitome of a sitting judge, Holmes remained very much the scholar in mood and outlook, if not in the depth of his researches or the frequency of his scholarly essays.[2] Because the thirty years after 1902 found him a member of the Supreme Court of the United States and almost immediately a major figure in American public life, a special effort may be required to appreciate both his accomplishments from 1883 to 1902 and the significance of these years in the development of his total outlook. As a judge his state court decisions were like flowers grown from the seeds cast down in *The Common Law*. Such an estimate need not be taken to imply that Holmes's generative intellect had reached a kind of plateau, however. The very opposite obtained. Though his writings for the bar and the informed public were to be less specialized as his opportunities for research narrowed under the burden of an impressive judicial workload, he continued to probe both the law and the cosmos, while offering some forward-looking opinions in cases which came before the Massachusetts high court. One of his most instructive essays, at once hardnosed and provocative, "The Path of the Law," was a product of these years. In it he contended, "If you want to know the law and nothing else, you must look at it as a bad man who cares only for the material consequences which such knowledge enables him to predict, not a good one, who finds his reasons for con-

70

duct, whether inside the law or outside of it, in the vaguer sanctions of conscience."[3] The law was "not a Hegelian dream, but part of the lives of men."[4] Yet two years prior to "The Path of the Law" Holmes had delivered his famous "The Soldiers' Faith." For high purpose, it is without equal in his writings. Part of a soldier's faith was "that the faith is truth and adorable which leads a soldier to throw away his life in obedience to a blindly accepted duty."[5] And among the lessons of war Holmes found that "high and dangerous action teaches us to believe as right beyond dispute things for which our doubting minds are also slow to find words of proof."[6] Sublime mysticism or errant nonsense, temperament, *zeitgeist,* or chemistry?

Whatever the temptation to make a judgment on the basis of isolated excerpts, such thoughts as Holmes expressed in his Memorial Day Address of 1884 or "The Soldiers' Faith" are essential for understanding the mature Holmes no less than "The Path of the Law" or "Learning and Science," writings of this period in which the empiricist spoke loudest. The evidence suggests that it was while on the Massachusetts bench that Holmes's mind gravitated, not in the direction of intellectual orthodoxy, but, more strangely still, toward a highly individualized mysticism. He arrived at such a position by his reflections on the Civil War. Memories of that struggle, of his part in it, and what it meant to him reasserted a belief that life in part was beyond human measurements. He spoke with regret of the passing of an age in which "the rainbow flush of cathedral windows, which once to enraptured eyes appeared the very smile of God, fade[d] slowly out into the pale irony of the void."[7] And of honor, even at the cost of death, he was moved to quote approvingly from Beowulf and from Tennyson who, in his own time, sang:

> Launch your vessel
> And crowd your canvas,
> And, ere it vanishes
> Over the margin,
> After it, follow it,
> Follow the Gleam.[8]

This is the same man, the same mind, which in "Law in Science and Science in Law" asserted that "it is finally for science to determine, as far as it can, the relative worth of our social end."[9]

Both sets of convictions are worthy of the mature Holmes, not in the sense that one cancels out the other, leaving an altogether ambiguous legacy, but rather in that he chose to accommodate both views in his own private thoughts about life and his judicial opinions on the law. The years from 1883 to 1902 mark the growth to intellectual fullness of a Holmes who, as associate justice of the Supreme Court of the United States, would be predictably unpredictable: now liberal, now conservative. Brooding on the Civil War experience—in afteryears he was the faithful veteran who was sure to remember anniversary dates of battles and to toast old wounds—brought him face to face once again with the mystery of life as with the uncertainties of death. As he was fond of saying, he held with Madame de Staël that while he did not believe in hell, he was afraid of it nevertheless. In any case, Holmes at times was prompted to reflect on the unknown aspects of life, beyond human knowledge and human understanding. "The law can ask no better justification than the deepest instincts of man," he wrote in "The Path of the Law."[10] Indeed, the mastery of law took a man outside himself in a sense, "straining those faculties by which man is likest to a god."[11] The high seriousness of purpose—Duty as he had discovered it in the Civil War—Holmes transmogrified fully and finally into a devotion to the Law. Belief in the Law had become for him another of those "can't helps," and thus a means of truth. Holmes could not help believe in "this abstraction called the Law, wherein, as in a magic mirror, we see reflected, not only our own lives, but the lives of all that men have been. When I think of this majestic theme, my eyes dazzle."[12]

II *Influences of* The Common Law

Evidence abounds of the direct translation of theories found in *The Common Law* into the opinions of Judge Holmes. To begin with, there was in his judicial decisions a distrust of generalities. "We think that the case at the bar [*Lorenzo* v. *Wirth* (1897–98)] is not beyond our competence to decide," he wrote in a majority opinion. "The greatest danger in attempting to do so is that of being misled by ready-made generalizations, and of thinking only in phrases to which as lawyers judges have been accustomed. . . . Too broadly generalized conceptions are a constant source of fallacy."[13] In another case, *Ryalls* v. *Mechanics Mills* (1889–90), Holmes argued that "general maxims are oftener an excuse for want of accurate analysis than a help in determining the extent of a duty or the construction of a statute.[14] Or again, in *Moran* v. *Dunphy* (1900–1901), he chided the court for "wasting time upon useless generalities about the construction of statutes."[15] This suspicion of general propositions was in keeping with Holmes's oft-expressed reservations about the value of philosophical speculations or absolutes in the practical processes of the law. "The law does not trouble itself very much with philosophic difficulties,"[16] as he once put it, so that it was "inexpedient and unjust to lay down a sweeping general principle. . . ."[17] Generalities simply had no place in law as part of the everyday lives of men.

This hostility to generalizations reflected itself in numerous ways, but especially in Holmes's individualized uses of truth. He wrote forcefully in this vein to Lady Pollock:

Well, to be civilized is to be potentially master of all possible ideas, and that means that one has got beyond being shocked, although one preserves one's own moral aesthetic preferences. I regard the latter, however, as more or less arbitrary, although none the less dogmatic on that account. Do you like sugar in your coffee or don't you? You admit the possibility of difference and yet are categorical in your own way, and even instinctively condemn those who do not agree. So as to truth. We tacitly postulate that if others were as intelligent and well educated as we they would be compelled to agree with us—but that is a mere ideal, not an actuality. They don't agree in fact. The fact is that each has his more or less differing system; whether there is an objective reality in which is to be found the unity of our several compulsions or whether our taste in truth is as arbitrary as our taste in coffee and there is no objective truth at all, I leave to philosophers by profession. I think the law is a better calling—though I used not to.[18]

Even so, "truth" could work hardship in a given set of circumstances. In *Hemenway* v. *Hemenway* (1883) Holmes took the position that "the court can hardly be asked to close its eyes upon the truth in order to lay down a rule which can only be justified on the grounds that it is beneficial."[19] At times the rough edges of life marked its reality, and Holmes was not likely to be dissuaded by the prospect of "doing good."

Similarly, Holmes spoke his doubts, if not his disdain, for moral rights:

> It must be remembered, [he wrote,] whenever a new statute comes up for consideration, that although it may be found by construction to give what it gives as if in pursuance of a legal duty, there is no such legal duty in fact, and no antecedent right on the part of the persons who receive its benefits. It is only tautologous to say that the law knows nothing of moral rights unless they are also legal rights, and from before the day of Hobbes the argument has been public property that there is no such thing as a right created by law, as against the sovereign who makes the law by which the right is to be created.[20]

Perhaps Holmes was less disdainful of moral rights than he was anxious to distinguish them from legal rights, which he considered the only legitimate interest of lawyers and judges.

This treatment of "moral rights" was in keeping with one of the main themes of *The Common Law*, the externalization of law. Put plainly, "as the aim of the law is not to punish sin, but it is to prevent certain external results, the act must come pretty near to accomplishing that result before the law will notice it."[21] This principle of externalization was forcefully illustrated in *Commonwealth* v. *Pierce* (1884–85). A physician prescribed that the clothes of a patient be kept saturated in kerosene as part of his medical treatment. The patient died and the doctor was sued for malpractice. The question of "moral recklessness," or the intention of the physician in his method of treatment, Holmes distinguished from recklessness according to the "external standards of what was morally reckless, under circumstances known to him [the doctor] as a man of reasonable prudence." Holmes reasoned further that neither idiosyncrasy nor good intention on the physician's part could be urged in his defense, and in concluding his argument invoked the external standard once more: "If the dangers are characteristic of the class according to the common experience, then he who uses an article of the class upon another can not escape on the ground that he had less than the common experience."[22] Holmes had not abandoned the moral law, as many would argue, but rather appealed to the moral law as it was approved and practiced by society at a given time. In so saying, he managed to embrace the newer version of truth as that which was workable, without severing workability from what history would have men believe was moral. In this light Holmes's jurisprudence appears less radical and less creative than "workability" implies, inasmuch as workability depends ultimately on what society has been taught—and continues to believe—is moral.

An interpretation of law which had only an external sanction was bound to have direct bearing on the way Holmes's opinions were framed in cases dealing with business. In *Clemens* v. *Walton* (1899), a case involving the sale of property, he argued coldly: "We agree that if the sale [of land] was in terms of votes, and those terms were legal, it would be none the worse that the transaction came very near to illegality, and was so framed as to avoid it."[23] In other words, nearness to illegality which carries at least a faint moral implication does not constitute violation of the law. The argument was more explicitly stated in *Hawkins* v. *Graham* (1889), which involved a dispute for the system of heating in a mill. "In view of modern modes of business," Holmes wrote, "it is not surprising that in some cases eager sellers should be found taking that degree of risk with unwilling purchasers. . . . We are of the opinion that the satisfactoriness of the system and the risk taken by the plaintiff were to be determined by the mind of a reasonable man, and by the external measures set forth in the contract, not by private taste or the liking of the defendant."[24] In a case involving the statute against fraud Holmes reminded the parties to the dispute that "a creditor has no private interest in a sentence, although it is incident to a proceeding in his private interest; and it is contrary to the analogies of the law to allow an appeal for the sole purpose of enhancing punishment."[25] If society was protected from the bad results of fraud, the law was satisfied. Law was not a question of enforcing the ethics of moral right and wrong, but a question of policy. And policy should be left as far as possible in the hands of the legislature.

The will of the legislature meant not only rule by the majority to Holmes but connoted the sovereign power of the state, of which a court was an arm. "If a competent court ... divorces a couple or establishes a will ... a paramount title is passed and the couple is divorced, the will is established, as against the world, whether parties or not, because the sovereign has said it shall be so."[26] Within the meaning of the sovereign power of the state, Judge Holmes justified restrictions on both property and personal rights. "It is plain that the right to use one's property for the sole purpose of injuring others is not one of the immediate rights of ownership; it is not a right for the sake of which property is recognized by the law, but it is only a more or less necessary incident of rights which are established for very different ends."[27] Again Holmes was found to quarrel with motive, expressing himself satisfied when property rights were restricted for the welfare of the community. It was the function of the courts to determine the balance of property rights with community needs. And if it be objected that such balancing became a matter of degree, Holmes assumed that when "nicely analyzed" most legal differences were a matter of degree.[28] As for free speech, it too might be limited. In *McAuliffe* v. *New Bedford* (1891–1892), Holmes ruled that a policeman might be dismissed from his job for violating a regulation aimed at political activity by a member of the force. "The petitioner may have a constitutional right to talk politics, but he has no constitutional right to be a policeman ... , he can not complain, as he takes the employment on the terms offered him."[29] The unifying principle which Holmes invoked was that the welfare of the community required—and rightly so—the sacrifice of individual prerogatives. This was a matter of practicality, and nothing more. "There are no sacramental words which must be used in a statutory power to take and hold lands," he wrote in City of *Newtown* v. *Perry* (1895).[30] "Higher laws" appeals were inappropriate to plaintiffs and defendants alike.

III   *State Decisions*

Before proceeding to a detailed consideration of several important cases in which Holmes had a part to play and a position to express, it may be useful to assess his record on the Massachusetts bench in somewhat general terms. Holmes did not dissent in writing from the majority in a case involving the Massachusetts Constitution until he had been on the court for five years. This does not prove that he never voted with the minority—since minority opinions were seldom written—but it does suggest that he did not feel impelled, either by his own judicial outlook or by the substance of the case at hand, to set down his own view of the law. Over the whole of his state court career, he voted with the majority four times out of five, and wrote one of every three majority opinions. Furthermore, about one in five of his opinions dealt with torts alone, as distinguished from cases in contract, criminal law, equity, and the like. The image emerges of a judge working patiently with the innumerable details of a legal system, glancing only occasionally at the broader outline and grand design of the constitution, of a judge who was dealing with the raw materials out of which a legal system arises and who sought to render that system intelligible from the ground up rather than the summit down.

In nearly twenty years of judging the law, and that in a state which had an advanced industrial society, a number of cases did arise, however, in which Holmes was called upon to help to decide important social questions. Several such cases, if reviewed in detail, may yield a better feeling for the work of Holmes as state court judge, especially as these cases foreshadow his widely known rulings as associate justice of the United States Supreme Court.

A series of suits came before the Supreme Judicial Court of Massachusetts in the 1890s which involved questions of management-labor conflicts. The issues were basic to employee rights in an industrial society, many of which were only then being defined at law in the states. In that area Massachusetts had already taken some initiatives, in 1887 passing an Employers' Liability Act, by which it "was settled law in Massachusetts that masters were personally bound to see that reasonable care was used to provide reasonably safe and proper machinery" in works and factories. The law stated further that the worker "himself be in exercise of due care." In *Ryalls* v. *Mechanics' Mills*, (1889–1890), the 1887 law was challenged. Holmes argued vigorously in its defense, content to accept the intention of the legislature as stated in the statute. In his view—expressed in a dissenting opinion—an injured employee "shall have the same right of compensation and remedies against the employer, as if he had not been an employee," and therefore had the right to sue an employer to collect damages if the latter were unwilling to comply freely with the law.[31]

An 1891 law, demonstrating further legislative concern for the protection of factory hands, stated that "no employer shall impose a fine or withhold wages or any part of wages of an employee engaged at weaving for imperfections that may arise during the process of weaving." Behind such a piece of legislation was widespread worker feeling that often managers alleged imperfections where there were none to defraud weavers of their earned wages. In *Commonwealth* v. *Perry* (1891), this law was brought to a constitutional test by a manufacturer who was found guilty in a lower court of actions contravening the law. A majority of the Supreme Court, hearing the case on appeal, found the law unconstitutional. The court based its opinion on Article I of the Declaration of Rights of the Massachusetts Constitution, which held that the "acquiring, possessing and protecting of property" was among the natural rights of men. The majority opinion stated that the manufacturing of cloth was an important industry in the state, in the operation of which contracts were essential; therefore, any statute which "forbids the making of such contracts, or attempts to nullify them, or impair them, violates fundamental principles of rights which are expressly recognized by our Constitution." Holmes's dissenting opinion was expressed in the plainest of language:

The statute cannot be said to impair the obligation of contracts made after it went into effect. . . . So far as has been pointed out to me, I do not see that it interferes with the right of acquiring, possessing, and protecting property any more than the laws against usury or gaming. In truth, I do not think that that clause of the Bill of Rights has any application. It might be urged, perhaps, that the power to make reasonable laws impliedly prohibits the making of unreasonable ones, and that this law is unreasonable. If I assume that this construction of the constitution is correct, and that, speaking as a political economist, I should agree in condemning the law, still I should not be willing or think myself authorized to overturn legislation on that ground, unless I thought that an honest difference of opinion was impossible, or pretty nearly so.

In offering this opinion, Holmes remarked that he thought it a "misfortune" that he had to differ from "my brethren," but went on to say that "considering the importance of the question, [I] feel bound to make public a brief statement, notwithstanding the respect and deference I feel for the judgment of those from whom I differ."[32] The first of his dissents on constitutional issues, it proved something of a portent.

Holmes had hardly broken a crusader's lance in favor of American labor in *Commonwealth* v. *Perry*, but his dissent revealed an unwillingness to see in every law favorable to labor's interest an assault on property. The opinion indicated that he was once again prepared to allow the legislative will to prevail in all but extraordinary circumstances.[33] His neutrality in the battle between managers and workers received a fresh challenge some five years later in the well-known case of *Vegelahn* v. *Guntner* (1896). Workers were engaged in picketing manufacturing establishments in order to try to prevent other workers from taking employment there, and thus winning certain concessions from management. The question at law was the right of a court to issue an injunction restraining the pickets. The majority of the court declared the picketing illegal and thus an injunction appropriate. Holmes, joined by Chief Justice Abner Field, dissented, supporting his position in part by reference to history and common sense.

It is plain from the slightest consideration of practical affairs, or the most superficial reading of industrial history, that free competition means combination, and that the organization of the world, now going on so fast, means an ever-increasing might and scope of combination. It seems to me futile to set our faces against this tendency. Whether beneficial on the whole, as I think it, or detrimental, it is inevitable, unless the fundamental axioms of society, and even the fundamental conditions of life, are to be changed.

One of the eternal conflicts out of which life is made up is that between the effort of every man to get the most he can for his services, and that of society, disguised under the name of capital, to get his services for the least possible return. Combination on the one side is patent and powerful. Combination on the other is the necessary and desirable counterpart, if the battle is to be carried on in a fair and equal way. . . .[34]

Methods of unionization were central to another case, *Plant* v. *Woods* (1900). Could a union recruit members from other unions by forcing employers—under threat of boycott and strike—to urge their workers to jump from one labor organization to another? The Massachusetts Supreme Judicial Court had granted an injunction denying this kind of activity, but before any boycott or strike had been commenced. The grounds of the injunction were that threats constituted coercion within the meaning of the law. Holmes's dissent in *Plant* v. *Woods* came as a reminder that he saw the distinction between a primary and a secondary boycott as a matter of degree, to be "nicely analyzed." He assumed that a majority of the court "would admit that a boycott or strike intended to raise wages might be lawful, if it did not embrace in its scheme or intent violence, breach of contract, or other unlawful conduct." The issue was thus narrowed to

the question whether, assuming that some purposes would be a justification, the purpose in this case of the threatened boycotts and strikers was such as to justify the threats. That purpose was not directly concerned with wages. It was one degree more remote. The immediate object and motive was to strengthen the defendants' society as a preliminary means to enable it to make a better fight on questions of wages or other matters of clashing interests. I differ from my brethren in thinking that the threats were as lawful for this preliminary purpose as for the final one to which strengthening the union was a means. I think that unity of organization is necessary to make the contest of labor effectual, and that societies of labor lawfully may employ in their preparation the means which they might use in the final contest.

Nor was Holmes reluctant to interpolate some of his economic thinking in the bargain.

While I think the strike is a lawful instrument in the universal struggle of life, I think it pure phantasy to suppose that there is a body of capital of which labor as a whole secures a larger share by that means. The annual product, subject to an infinitesimal deduction for the luxuries of the few, is directed to consumption by the multitude, and is consumed by the multitude, always. Organizations and strikers may get a larger share for the members of an organization, but, if they do, they get it at the expense of the less organized and less powerful portion of the laboring mass. They do not create something out of nothing. It is only by divesting our minds of ownership and other machinery of distribution, and by looking solely at the question of consumption,—asking ourselves what is the annual product, who consumes it, and what changes would or could we make,—that we can keep in the world of realities.[35]

Taken together, the thrust of these opinions dealing with industrial disputes and conflicts pointed to the new century in which the increasing size and complexity of the economic order would make attractive a political philosophy of a neutral, nationalist state.

In a variety of considerations which came before the Supreme Judicial Court while Holmes was on that bench, other signs of the new century and the changes in society it signified became evident. In 1892, for example, the state legislature sought an advisory opinion from the court as to the constitutionality of a law empowering municipalities to buy and sell fuel and to maintain fuel yards. Might not a commodity like coal be treated as any public utility? Cooperative efforts of a number of different kinds were being experimented with in western states especially. The general public could well benefit from this and similar municipal enterprises, but the anticapitalistic bent of such a proposal was obvious. A majority of the court ruled that the scheme was "bad law" on the grounds that "the Constitution does not contemplate this as one of the ends for which government was established." Judge Barker, along with Holmes, thought otherwise. "In my opinion," the latter wrote, "when money is taken to enable a public body to offer to the public without discrimination an article of general necessity, the purpose is no less public when that article is wood or coal than when it is water, or gas, or electricity, or education, to say nothing of cases like the support of paupers or the taking of land for railroads or public markets."[36]

Another advisory opinion in which Holmes disagreed with the court majority was *In re Municipal Suffrage to Women* 1894). The Commonwealth's legislature sought advice on whether or not "an act granting to women the right to vote in town and city elections" was constitutional, if it provided that "such an act shall take effect throughout the commonwealth upon its acceptance by a majority of the voters of the whole commonwealth." The majority had advised that such an act was against the Constitution inasmuch as it amounted to an abdication by the legislature of its prescribed power. Holmes's position is of interest because, paradoxically, it affirmed and denied the power of the legislature. The legislature might "exercise its discretion by taking the opinion of its principal, if it thinks that course is wise," was Holmes's way of summarizing his view. He then proceeded to sound a clear and less ambiguous note by scoring the majority view of the court as "an echo of Hobbes' theory that the surrender of the sovereignty by the people was final," noting that the case cited by his brother judges used "theory in language which is almost borrowed from the *Leviathan*." The Populist-Progressive tone sounded louder as Holmes argued in support of "local option," for in such a question the people might well be canvassed at the grass roots.[37]

Commonwealth v. *Davis* (1895) was a case at law involving a Boston city ordinance which prohibited public addresses on public grounds without a permit from the mayor. Holmes, speaking for the majority, found the law constitutionally valid. The ordinance was not aimed at free speech, but "in fact is directed toward the modes in which Boston Common may be used." As a representative of the public, it [the city] may and does exercise control over the use which the public may make of such places. ... For the legislature absolutely or conditionally to forbid public speaking in a highway or public park is no more an infringement of the rights of a member of the public than for the owner of a private house to forbid it in his house."[38]

IV *Philosopher Judge*

In the midst of all this court work Holmes's mind continued to hunger for a greater variety of food than ever the law could provide. He was rereading Hobbes' *Leviathan* in 1893, as well as "Karl Marx's book," observing of the latter that "although he strikes me as a great man I can't imagine a combination less to my taste than Hegel and political economy."[39] These same years found him "delving in some philosophy (especially Windelband's *History of Philosophy*), novels, and confusing arguments on bi-metallism."[40] Despite occasional outings to the theater—Sarah Bernhardt in the *Dame aux Camelias*, for example—he summed his days as "living like a recluse and working hard, just hard enough, that is. Solitude, socialism, and solitaire."[41] And of course, his ongoing correspondence with Frederick Pollock.

For all his tolerance and forward-looking ideas, there were few occasions for Holmes in his capacity of sitting judge to probe the mysteries of man and the universe. At bench and bar the law was too often "the laborious study of a dry and technical system, the greedy watch for clients and practice of shopkeepers' arts, the mannerless conflicts over often sordid interests."[42] Recognizing this, he continued to write scholarly pieces for the journals and to give inspirational speeches to private and public gatherings in which he unveiled both a respect for the scientific and an earnest wonderment regarding the cosmos. Here the interplay of the empirical and the mystical was sometimes enunciated but more often adumbrated in telling phrase, as Holmes spoke of "wearing his heart out after the unattainable,"[43] "lay[ing] his course by a star he has never seen."[44] The center of his mysticism was the Law.

To the lover of the law, how small a thing seem the novelist's tales of the loves and fates of Daphnis and Chloe! How pale a phantom even the Circe of poetry, transforming mankind with intoxicating dreams of fiery ether, and the foam of summer sea, and glowing greensward, and the white arms of women! For him no less a history will suffice than that of the moral life of his race. For him every text that he deciphers, every doubt that he resolves, adds a new feature to the unfolding panorama of man's destiny upon this earth. Nor will his task be done until, by the farthest stretch of human imagination, he has seen as with his eyes the birth and growth of society, and by the farthest stretch of reason he has understood the philosophy of its being. When I think thus of the law, I see a princess mightier than she who once wrought at Bayeaux, eternally weaving into her web dim figures of the ever-lengthening past,—figures too dim to be noticed by the idle, too symbolic to be interpreted except by her pupils, but to the discerning eye disclosing every painful step and every worldshaking contest by which mankind has worked and fought its way from savage isolation to organic social life.[45]

Holmes's writings and speeches over the full span of his state judgeship exhibited the empirical and the mystical in less than equal measure, because more often than not he was dealing with the technicalities of the law. For example, he wrote six major pieces for law journals, beginning with "Early English Equity," published in the *Law Review Quarterly* in 1885. Two lengthy articles on "Agency" were followed by essays on "Privilege, Malice and Intent," "Executors," and "Legal Interpretations"—all these latter items appearing in the *Harvard Law Review*. Whatever the demands of the bench upon his time and energy, Holmes had not yet done with legal scholarship unrelated to specific cases and official court opinion. In "Early English Equity" he set about to investigate "uses," the "parent of our modern trusts," which he termed "the greatest contribution to the substantive law which has ever been set down to the credit of the Chancery."[46] In the process he was to show that substantive law was not "the product of procedure, and did not embody superior ethical standards."[47] "Uses," as a reading of history demonstrated, developed from German and English practices which seemed appropriate to the needs of earlier times. Holmes declared the doctrine of uses "as little the creation of the subpoena, or of degrees requiring personal obedience, as it was an improvement invented in a relatively high state of civilization which the common law was too archaic to deal with."[48] "Early English Equity" was a scholar's understanding of complex and somewhat obscure legal origins consistent with Holmes's general effort to justify legal uses as the outgrowth of custom and not procedure.

In his treatment of "Agency" the judge recurred to one of his favorite themes of *The Common Law*: how legal practices, which arose from social conditions that had since altered if not disappeared in the modern period, had been "generalized into a fiction. Although nothing in the world but a form of words, such practices reacted upon the law and tended to carry its anamolies still further."[49] Leading his readers on an extensive and erudite exploration of the development of "Agency" from the Romans to eighteenth-century English legal history, Holmes's main purpose was simple: "to show that the whole outline of the law, as it stands today, is the resultant of a conflict between logic and good sense—the one striving to carry fictions out to consistent results, the other restraining and at last overcoming that effort when the results become too manifestly unjust."[50] Holmes was ready to admit that "the views here maintained are not favorites with the courts," a fact which he knew well enough from first hand experience. And he was ready to parody those judges who had to admit that they might have to find defendants guilty because of a fiction of law.[51]

In "Privilege, Malice and Intent," several of Holmes's favorite contentions surfaced. One of these was that of the external legal standards.[52] The law is indifferent, at least in torts if not in criminal proceedings, whether an act is one of malice or negligence, he argued.[53] Another favorite proposition was that privileges in such matters were questions of legislative policy,[54] questions furthermore which "cannot be answered by generalities but must be determined by the particular character of the case. . . ."[55] Finally Holmes took aim at jurists who were reluctant to "leave the path of merely logical deduction . . . to lose the illusion of certainty which makes legal reason seem like mathematics,"[56] as well as those who, when the issues were "social," were willing to depart from their own logic and to embark on questions of policy which rightly belong to legislative bodies. As for such efforts as the prevention of labor combination, Holmes thought the courts were "flying in the face of the organization of the world which is taking place so fast, and of its inevitable consequences."[57] He added that his purpose was not merely to criticize decisions but to call attention to the "very serious legislative considerations which have to be weighed."[58] Taken together all these scholarly essays are best viewed as extensions and elaborations of *The Common Law*. They echoed the protests against generalizations and entered pleas in the name of the externalization of the law.

V   *Holmes the Preacher*

The parallels among *The Common Law*, Holmes's court opinions, and his legal scholarship were hardly unexpected. A more intriguing question is whether such similarities were sustained in his general writings and his notable addresses during the years from 1883 to 1902, or whether his ideas, depending on his topic, were diluted by an instinct for cosmic wondering about the Law, about Truth, about Life itself. The range of his efforts in any case was impressive: from an article in *Youth's Companion* called "The Bar as a Profession," to "The Path of the Law," one of his better-known statements of the predictive thesis, from the ingenuous to the more subtle shading of legal theory. Holmes showed himself still in pursuit of some acceptable accommodation of positivism and traditionalism which gives to any expression of his mind a dimension of allure and an excitement which would not obtain had he been indulging in mere theorizing. Indeed, one of the attractive elements in what Holmes wrote and spoke about was his involvement in the ideas he enunciated and thus the persuasion which typically became part of his effect on people.

On few if any topics could Holmes wax as persuasive as on the Civil War. Indelible memories of his part in that struggle he evoked with rare candor in a Memorial Day Address in 1884.[59] The remarks offered were much like a stream of consciousness, disclosing that he found comfort and solace in the certainties surrounding Duty in war and the real demands it made on men. He posed the question: why keep Memorial Day at all?[60] As a challenge this question was not directed at those soldiers who had served, North and South, for they never questioned their sacred Duty. Rather it was aimed at those who did not share the soldiers' experiences and the memories. The answers which Holmes gave were striking. But he must be allowed to speak for himself. Memorial Day, he said, "solemnly affirms from year to year a national act of enthusiasm and faith," because "to fight a war you must believe in something and want something with all your might."[61] The Judge quite frankly celebrated the good effect of war on the individual soldier, calling its memorials "worth more to our young men by way of chastening and inspiration than the monuments of another hundred years of peaceful life could be."[62] The romance, the mysticism of the speaker, glowed with an incandescence as he told of meeting old comrades at annual encampments of the Grand Army of the Republic and of recalling old comrades never to be met again because they had died heroes: the brave captain, the fair lieutenant, men of "high breeding, romantic chivalry." "We who have seen these men can never believe that the power of money or the enervation of pleasure has put an end to them. We know that life may still be lifted into poetry and lit with spiritual charm."[63] Speaking for others, but especially for himself, Holmes told poignantly of "the generation that carried on the war [as] . . . set apart by its experiences. Through our great good fortune, in our youth our hearts were touched with fire. It was given to us to learn at the outset that life is a profound and passionate thing."[64] One man's mysticism may be another man's foolishness, to be sure; mystic experience defies language, as it defies time. But there can be no mistaking the message which Holmes set out to convey, his belief in something beyond the self, a belief which was natural to man, belief in a cause, a nation, an ideal. Furthermore, it was a belief one "can't help" embracing. Though he was not often given to such moods, their rare presence may be taken as a clue, nonetheless, of the authenticity of the spiritual Holmes.

Though the occasion was different, the sentiments which Holmes offered in his address "The Use of Law Schools" were kindred. He had been invited by the Harvard Law School Association to address that body as part of the celebration surrounding the 250th Aniversary of Harvard University in 1886. He told his fellows that "nearly all the education which men can get from others is moral, not intellectual," while "the main part of intellectual [education] is not the acquisition of facts, but learning how to make facts live."[65] He expressed his concern over the bad effects of democracy, because as it was progressing in America it tended to deny the distinctions between individuals which were founded in Nature itself: "Morality and reverence are no less virtues of freemen than the democratic feeling which will submit neither to arrogance nor to servility."[66] The aim of a law school ought to be to teach its students "the union of democracy and discipline," their duty that of "the service of Truth, their only queen."[67] That pursuit of truth in law was now being aided by "science . . . gradually drawing legal history into its sphere."[68] Such a development only altered the method of serving Truth, Holmes preferring wisdom to "smartness," and hoping that Harvard would not only teach the law, but teach it in the grand manner.[69] "The best part of our education is moral," he concluded, which was the "glory of this Law School," having enkindled "in many a heart an inextinguishable flame."[70]

This speech was typical of Holmes the preacher. Certain that men must have passion and commitment, discipline and values, and that they must be animated by these elements, he remained vague as to the nature of truth. His dilemma was not uncharacteristic of a generation which was close enough to the age of faith to want the reassurances of simple beliefs, but far too scientific to be willing to define this ancient urge.

> A moth between a window and a star
> Not wholly lured by one or led by the other.[71]

But for such as Holmes it remained unnecessary to define his ultimate. It was enough to know there was one, a viewpoint he put so well in his 1897 Commencement Address at Brown University:

I care not very much for the form if in some way he [the graduate] has learned that he cannot set himself over against the universe as a rival god, to criticise it, or shake his fist at the skies, but that his meaning is its meaning, his only worth is a part of it, as a humble instrument of the universal power.[72]

Such a passage was typical of Holmes the cosmic wonderer.

Holmes continued his wondering in "The Soldiers' Faith,"[73] an 1895 Harvard address. War had surely scraped his mind with its jagged edges, yet somehow war was good for the race. War for men, motherhood for women—sources of ideals for the species—this inheritance Holmes doubted "we are ready to give up."[74] Admitting again that he did not know the meaning of the universe, he remained certain of the value of duty in war. Deeds of valor went against common sense, but men were able to put common sense aside to die for a great cause: "Man had in him that unspeakable somewhat which makes him capable of a miracle, able to lift himself by the might of his own soul, unaided, able to face annihilation for a blind belief." Time in its passage reveals that the message of war is divine.[75] Attacking the materialism of his era as he discovered it in "this smug oversafe corner of the world," America, he dissented from the "individualist negation . . . revolting at discipline, loving flesh-pots, and denying that anything is worthy of reverence."[76] But for all of this, a touch of social Darwinist ethics intruded, as Holmes told his audience that "if once in a while in our rough riding a neck is broken, I regret it not as a waste, but as a price well paid for the breeding of a race fit for leadership and command."[77] And at the close of the address the speaker added a note of fatalism. His old regiment had shrunk to a skeleton, a ghost, a memory. It should be so, he thought, so that one is left to wonder not about the "true Holmes" but about his changing moods.[78]

VI *Of Two Minds*

It must be clear that, when he moved away from the Law, Holmes was a curious mix of the old truths and the new scientific mentality. But when he addressed himself to the Law, he was much more the proponent of new thought evolving from the old but not bound or limited by it. In *The Path* "of the Law," an address at the Boston University Law School in 1897, his predictive theory had a full statement.[79] The object of his study was "prediction, the prediction of the incidence of public force through the instruments of the courts."[80] Moving a step forward he showed that "a legal duty so-called is nothing but a prediction that if a man does or omits certain things he will be made to suffer in this way or that way by judgment of the court; and so of legal right."[81] Thus he proceeded to state what has become that classic Holmesian passage: "The prophecies of what the courts will do in fact, and nothing more pretentious, are what I mean by the law."[82] He was again outspoken in his protest of legal rules which simply persisted "from blind imitation of the past."[83] Holmes was one with Havelock Ellis, holding that "not the nature of the crime, but the dangerousness of the criminal, constitutes the only reasonable legal criterion to guide the inevitable social reaction against the criminal."[84] These and a dozen like contentions were part of *The Path* "of the Law." Yet at the close Holmes allowed himself a moment of speculation: "General aspects of the law are those which give it universal interest. It is through them that you not only become a great master in your calling, but connect your subject with the universe and catch an echo of the infinite, a glimpse of its unfathomable process, a hint of the universal law."[85]

Reliance on science was the feature of Holmes's "Law in Science and Science in Law," an address before the Bar Association of the State of New York in 1899.[86] The really important part of the true science of law, he thought, "consists in the establishment of its postulates from within upon accurately measured social desires instead of tradition."[87] Human actions in turn became amoral: "The theory of law as to any possible conduct is that it is either lawful or unlawful."[88] Even so—

In law we only occasionally can reach an absolutely final and quantitative determination, because of the worth of competing social ends which respectively solicit a judgment for the plaintiff or the defendant cannot be reduced to number and accurately fixed. The worth, that is, the intensity of the competing desires, varies with the varying ideals of the time, and, if the desires were constant, we could not get beyond a relative decision that one was greater and one was less. But it is of the essence of improvement that we should be as accurate as we can.[89]

And so Holmes, the scientist in the Law, drew back, at the last moment, from the logical consequences of science because the human situation with its "competing desires" and "varying ideals" required it.

A peculiarity characteristic of Holmes is now visible. When he took up the themes of Duty or Truth, he felt the need to insert a warning, a corrective, perhaps, that such ideals were not uninfluenced by scientific modes of thought, and should in fact be weighed in a scientific balance. When, in contrast, he was busy analyzing the place and function of science in law, he did not choose to ignore the limitations on science imposed by the human condition. Holmes in both instances revealed something akin to a compulsion to cut across the grain of his major argument at a crucial point, leaving on the retina of history a double image, that of liberal and conservative.

A useful final statement on the mind of Holmes in the years before he advanced to the Supreme Court in Washington occurs in remarks before the Boston Bar in March of 1900 as he spoke sensitively of his position and his posture.[90] Holmes offered what he called "the triune formula of the joy, the duty, and the end of life."[91] And he went on:

It was of this that Malebranche was thinking when he said that, if God held in one hand truth, and in the other the pursuit of truth, he would say: "Lord, the truth is for thee alone; give me the pursuit." The joy of life is to put out one's power in some natural and useful or harmless way. There is no other. And the real misery is not to do this.[92]

Confessing his belief that altruism and selfish cynicism were "about equally unreal" and that loving one's neighbor was a vain attempt at life, Holmes insisted that this motto was "Whatsoever thy hand findeth to do, do it with thy might."[93] To him, that rule was infinitely important.

CHAPTER 5

The Progressive Era: Interpretations

I Appointed to Supreme Court

OLIVER Wendell Holmes was sworn in as an associate justice of the United States Supreme Court on December 8, 1902. In that same month he wrote to Pollock:

Yes—here I am—more absorbed, interested, and impressed than ever I had dreamed I might be. The work of the past seems a finished book—locked up far away, and a new and solemn volume opens. The variety and novelty of the questions, the remote spaces from which they come, the amount of work they require, all help the effect.[1]

In his later phrase, he was "in fresh fields and pastures new now," experiencing a strange but satisfying exhilaration in the husbandry of the federal law.[2]

A number of factors entered into the Holmes Supreme Court appointment. He had gained the reputation as a reformer while on the Massachusetts bench, and Theodore Roosevelt, a Progressive president, was anxious to have such a man named to the Court. Furthermore, his appointment was urged strenuously by Henry Cabot Lodge, senator from Massachusetts and a friend of both Holmes and the president. Finally, Holmes's distinguished name and his Civil War record appeared to make his choice the right one on every count. Holmes was not himself a Progressive, however.[3] Achieving national prominence by virtue of many judicial opinions which became part of the Progressive faith and legacy, he interpreted the law by norms largely innocent both of Progressive aspirations and the politics which gave them birth. All of this is not to argue that he was un-Progressive, much less anti-Progressive, but to assert the uniqueness of

92

Holmes as he judged cases which came before the High Court during the Progressive years. The distinction between Holmes's outlook and that of Progressives is best understood in light of his "intent." In his interpretations he did not consciously seek to hand down Progressive opinions. Although many of his decisions coincided with Progressive preferences in the law and the Constitution, it can not be assumed from that fact that Holmes was a reformer. Coincidence is not causality.

II *Intellectual Profile*

In such cases where Holmes displayed a concern for social welfare, for example, the origin of his interpretation might be pragmatism. Paraphrasing Charles S. Peirce's admittedly awkward but widely recognized definition of pragmatic truth, Holmes asks us to "consider what effects that might conceivably have practical bearings, we conceive the law to have on society; then the effects of that law are the sum total of its validity, rendering it good or bad." Such a statement may very well serve as a practical rule for appreciating certain of Holmes's constitutional interpretations. Unlike Peirce, however, who operated in the realm of theory, Holmes's rulings dealt with society and social requirements. To estimate the effects of a law as good or bad for society demanded that he implicitly exercise moral judgments as to right or wrong, his particular notion of what he understood society was willing to treat as right or wrong. Nor on occasion did Holmes claim less than this. In the case *Coppage* v. *Kansas* (1914),[4] which dealt with a worker discharged for union membership, Holmes found that "in present conditions a workman not unnaturally may believe that only by belonging to a union can he secure a contract that shall be fair to him.... If that belief, whether right or wrong, may be held by a reasonable man, it seems to me that it may be enforced by law in order to establish the equality of position between the two parties in which liberty of contract begins." To which he added: "see further Vegelahn v. Guntner,... Plant v. Woods.... I still entertain the opinions expressed by me in Massachusetts." Though appearing not to do so, Holmes had interpolated into his dissenting opinion in *Coppage* v. *Kansas* a moral element, social rather than individual in nature. This was the kind of ruling which made him both a respected jurist and a popular judge, since he composed in a single judgment the scientific and the traditional points of view.

As one charged with interpreting the Constitution of the United States, during the Progressive Era Holmes came face to face with what had been one of his main objections to law traditionally conceived, that is, rule by the dead hand of the past. Should a modern industrial society of 100 million citizens be governed by a document and early court rulings which were better identified with the eighteenth and nineteenth centuries than with the twentieth? Holmes was eager to participate in an updating of the supreme law of the land: "The provisions of the Constitution are not mathematical formulas, having their form," he observed; "they are organic living institutions transplanted from English soil. Their significance is vital not formal; it is to be gathered not simply by taking the words and a dictionary, but by considering their origin and the line of their growth."[5] Behind such a resounding argument stood Holmes's conviction as to the nature of law, and not a commitment to any sort of Progressive creed.

Holmes also brought to his Supreme Court opinions an endorsement of elements of social Darwinism. At times this translated itself into a simple recognition that society as it had evolved had grown more complex, more interdependent, and therefore more delicately poised. In addition, evolution implied the possibility of changes in the location of power, as well as an increase in strength according to the rule of survival of the fittest. Such a consideration might dictate major shifts in socioeconomic organization in the United States. Holmes's opinion in the *Northern Securities* case of 1904 was premised on the principle that great size was a natural and necessary consequence of growth with which it might not be wise to tamper. "Size in the case of railroads," he wrote, "is an inevitable incident. . . . In the case of railroads it is evident that the size of the combination is reached for other ends than those which would make them monopolies."[6] His attitude in the *Lochner* decision of 1905, in contrast, intimated that an altered relationship between capital and labor was in the offing. He rejected a majority opinion which issued from "an economic theory that a large part of the country does not entertain," that the "Fourteenth Amendment does not enact Mr. Herbert Spencer's Social Statics."[7] It was the duty of the judges who made the law to rule according to the realities, and not according to theories.

Another factor influencing Holmes's High Court rulings was his perennial respect for the will of the legislature, which combined naturally with his distrust of general propositions in the law. Two early cases during his Court tenure illustrated his attachment to these principles. In *Otis* v. *Parker* (1902) he argued a majority view, noting that

it is true, no doubt, that neither a State legislature nor a State constitution can interfere arbitrarily with private business. . . . But general propositions do not carry us far.[8]

The next year, 1904, he stated his position again in *Missouri, Kansas, and Texas Ry. Co.* v. *May*:

When a State legislature has declared that in its opinion policy requires a certain measure, its actions should not be disturbed by the courts under the Fourteenth Amendment, unless they clearly see that there is no fair reason for the law. . . . Great constitutional provisions must be administered with caution.[9]

Judicial restraint had won a voice in the rulings of the new associate justice from Massachusetts.

Akin to this emphasis on the prerogatives of legislatures was Holmes's celebration of the sovereign power of the state. As he once insisted to Laski, whatever we might think of the personality of man as an individual, "the Sovereign state kills him when it sees fit and can."[10] In *Missouri* v. *Holland* (1920), an opinion on which he "worked fiercely," Holmes described the nature and the extent of American national sovereignty.[11] The case concerned a treaty between Great Britain and the United States over the control of migratory birds; certain provisions of the treaty conflicted with a statute of the state of Missouri. In defending the sovereignty inhering in the nation, Holmes contended that treaties were the supreme law of the land when made under the

authority of the United States, that the United States possessed
the authority which resided in every civilized government, that
is, the ultimate power to command its citizens or its component
parts (the states). When dealing with a constituent act, like the
Constitution,

> we must realize that they [the Founding Fathers] have called into
> life a being the development of which could not have been forseen
> completely by the most gifted of the begetters. It was enough for
> them to realize or to hope that they had created an organism; it has
> taken a century and cost their successors much sweat and blood to
> prove that they have created a Nation. . . . Here a national interest
> of very nearly the first magnitude is involved. It can be protected
> only by national action in concert with another great power.[12]

This line of argument led unerringly to the principle that "the
foundation of jurisdiction is physical power," a teaching Holmes
had long advocated.[13]

There is still another angle for viewing Holmes's interpretations of the law. His personal tastes, taken in the ethical sense of
the word, sometimes became the determinant of his judicial conclusions. Dissent in *Hammer* v. *Dagenhart* (1918), the child
labor case, is a prime example.[14] "If there is any matter upon
which civilized countries have agreed—far more unanimously
than they have with regard to intoxicants and some other matters
over which this country is now emotionally aroused," he observed, "—it is the evil of premature and excessive child labor. I
should have thought that if we were to introduce our own moral
conceptions where in my opinion they do not belong, this was
preeminently a case for upholding the exercise of all its powers
by the United States." Holmes went on to speak of the goods
made by child labor as "the product of ruined lives." Clearly he
was offended by child labor, and spoke his mind in an idiom
not unlike that of John Spargo's *Bitter Cry of the Children*. As
reluctant as he remained to intrude his own sensitivities into the
law, occasions could arise in which he chose not to do otherwise.
He would have disclaimed the label of Progressive, nonetheless,
ensconced as he was on Olympus and indifferent to the ebb and
flow of political vogues.

Pragmatism, legal and judicial caveats, theories of the state, social Darwinism, and moral tastes were the general guidelines according to which Holmes's interpretations of the Constitution and the law were offered. They were conditioning factors, philosophical presuppositions essential to Holmes's thought, sometimes articulated, often silent, but consistently a part of the justice's outlook. President Roosevelt indeed had named a brilliant legal personality to the Supreme Court. This brilliance only thinly masked a complex, paradoxical, restless mind, original, individualistic, and, in a parallel sense, as Progressive as any justice of the times.

III *Holmes's Washington*

The Washington to which Holmes came in December of 1902 was alive with excitement. Politics had suddenly gained a new respectability to accompany its aura of drama with Theodore Roosevelt in the White House. Roosevelt was the man of the hour. He filled up the presidency with a contagious love of life and power, and on the strength of his first year in office gave every indication of utilizing the executive authority to bring about long-needed reforms. The times were ripe for such a man, and the man very nearly perfect for the times. America had entered upon a new century, full of hope and promise, if a proper orchestration of capital and labor, of resources and their use, of moral fervor and social requirements could be achieved. While initiatives for reform would come from the president and the Progressive leaders in the Congress, the Supreme Court would have a special role to play. The Court, long suspicious of laws tampering with the status quo and quick to invoke the Fourteenth Amendment to stem the tide of change and preserve the rights of property, deserved its reputation as a conservative bastion. Unless the Court was ready to embrace a more liberal doctrine, progress must remain unrealized. When Holmes came on the bench only Justice Harlan was prepared to move in the direction of liberal nationalism. Chief Justice Fuller and Associate Justices Brewer and Shiras, for example, were staunch in their defense of property rights. Other justices, while occasionally prepared to support reform measures like the income tax law, were nevertheless basically conservative. Holmes's appointment

was intended to inject a liberal note into Supreme Court deliber-
ations. But he confessed to Pollock at midpoint in the Progressive Era, he was "rather skeptical about reforms."[15] His appointment was not ill-advised, as it turned out; it was merely fortuitous
for the work of reform on the part of the judiciary. But such
thoughts as Holmes expressed to Pollock in 1909 were locked in
the future. For the moment, in 1902, he was exuberant, and
deeply aware of the responsibilities of his new position.

When Holmes arrived in Washington there stood that exclusive
circle of men, in and out of government, who cared deeply about
America and who attempted to explain the greatness of their
country on the one hand and to chart its future on the other:
Mahan, Hay, and Brooks Adams among them. The younger
Adams in particular had been influenced by Holmes's sociological
approach to jurisprudence. He had been among those who, in
the company of young Louis Brandeis, had come to listen and
to learn in the gas-lighted auditorium of the Lowell Institute.
True, the tendency of Holmes to apply scientific concepts to
history and to law was part of the intellectual climate in England
and in America, but it was Holmes who perhaps had the most
far-reaching effect on Adams's understanding of law as a product
of custom. When Adams brought out *Law of Civilization and
Decay*, Holmes was greatly impressed, referring to it as "the
most immediately interesting history I ever read."[16] No doubt
Brooks Adams's brand of cynicism appealed to what Holmes admitted was his "malevolent fancy."[17] But he was not always
prepared to follow where Adams chose to lead, however intellectually suggestive many of his notions were.[18] Misgivings apart,
Holmes welcomed the camaraderie of such as Adams once he
was settled in Washington. They shared an intellectual awareness
with people who controlled the affairs, and quite possibly the
destiny, of the American Republic.[19]

Under the driving influence of Theodore Roosevelt, the country by 1903 was assuming more and more a Progressive outlook.[20]
Stated simply, the reformers wanted to make politics honest and
efficient, the economy fair and just, and society open and equita-
ble. Specifically, the great power of the industrial trusts had to
be curbed, rendering them more socially valuable without requiring them to forego profits. The main body of reform opinion

was that conservative and that sincere. The Sherman Anti-Trust Act of 1890 had proved no more than an empty gesture in placating public distrust of corporate power. Whatever promise it held had been frustrated by the Supreme Court's attitude beginning with the *E. C. Knight* case of 1895, which said the sugar monopoly did not violate the law. To most reformers and to Roosevelt especially, the trusts were the vital center of corruption. Their immense power enabled them to debauch the body politic—Roosevelt considered the bribe whether given or taken as the greatest sin a public man could commit—and at the same time deluge the market with shoddy goods, dangerous drugs, and poisonous foods. His war on the trusts was therefore not merely a determination to display presidential power flamboyantly; it was predicated on a conviction that by reducing the trusts to a condition of responsibility to the public, the log-jam blocking a wide-ranging reform program would be broken. For the political branches of the national government, this called for a reinterpretation of their constitutional powers in light of accumulating social grievances which the national government alone possessed the power to redress. Proposals for the bold assertion of congressional and presidential initiatives grew out of a conviction that the Constitution was not a static charter of government but an instrument of self-government which had to be redefined by each generation according to the realities of each age. The constitutional means were at hand, as for example in the commerce clause, which would enable the national government to exercise important police power. Acceptance of this new version of federal authority—liberal nationalism—by the Supreme Court was essential to the whole movement, however. Roosevelt had appointed Holmes to the Court in order to help promote liberal nationalism within the judiciary, presuming that on the great public issues of the day their views were kindred. His vote with the majority in the two earliest cases upholding federal police power, *Champion* v. *Ames* (1903) and *McCray* v. *United States* (1904), dealing with lotteries and oleomargarine, respectively, appeared to vindicate the President's choice. Holmes's dissent in the *Northern Securities* case (1904) was, in consequence, all the more surprising.

IV   *The Northern Securities Case*

Holmes's "un-Progressive" dissent in *Northern Securities Company* v. *United States*, and thus his break with Roosevelt in this very important test of strength between the government and the corporations, gains added meaning because of the politics surrounding the origin and prosecution of the giant railroad combination. The Northern Securities Corporation was a holding company for the Northern Pacific, the Great Northern, and the Chicago, Burlington and Quincy railroad lines. J. P. Morgan, James J. Hill, E. H. Harriman, and the Rockefeller interests were committed to this scheme, which sought to monopolize the railroad business of the Pacific Northwest and thus gain a dominant position in the economy of that fast developing region. It had been capitalized at $400 million, an estimated one-third of which was watered stock. Because of its size, the names associated with the venture, and the stakes involved, the Northern Securities Corporation easily figured as a symbol of business power and the arrogance of a plutocracy which continued to hold the public be damned. Roosevelt saw the company as a tailor-made target, ideal for opening his war on the trusts. Despite the far-reaching implications of his move, he decided not to consult party leaders in the Congress before acting. Instead, he surprised the country when he ordered Attorney General Philander C. Knox to commence the suit without forewarning. Papers were filed in federal court in St. Paul, Minnesota, in March of 1902, government attorneys contending that the holding company was in restraint of trade between the states in violation of the Sherman Act. The president's action was part of the "square deal" he had promised the American people. If the stock market was deeply disturbed by the government suit, the public applauded a chief executive who was prepared to defy the tycoons. The easy relationship of government and business was at an end. Morgan's suggestion that he send his man to meet with Roosevelt's man to "fix up" the matter only exacerbated the situation. It was against this background that Holmes was named to the Supreme Court, T.R. convinced of the wisdom of his choice by the judge's record on the Massachusetts bench, where his rulings had been criticized by railroad executives and corporation men generally. In short,

Roosevelt expected Holmes to do his duty. He had laid out his views to Henry Cabot Lodge, the influential Massachusetts senator who had supported Holmes's appointment to the Supreme Court:

> In the ordinary and low sense which we attach to the words "partisan" and "politician," a judge of the Supreme Court should be neither. But in the higher sense he is not in my judgment fitted for the position unless he is a party man, a constructive statesman, keeping in mind his relations with his fellow statesmen in other branches of the Government.[21]

The president's disappointment in Holmes's dissent from a majority opinion which upheld the government's contention is understandable.

The majority opinion in the *Northern Securities* case was written by Justice Harlan. He denied the corporation's contention that since the holding company was essentially a stock transaction it had nothing to do with commerce. The corporation, in consequence, so the argument went, was not within the meaning of the Sherman Act's prohibition on restraint of "trade." In what amounted to a reversal of *United States* v. *E. C. Knight* of 1895, Harlan judged the Sherman Act applicable to both stock transactions and possibly manufacturing forms which operated in restraint of trade. Nor was Harlan willing to accept the corporation's position that the Sherman Act violated the reserve powers of the Tenth Amendment. This would have meant, he argued, "nothing less than that Congress, in regulating interstate commerce, must act in subordination to the will of the states when exercising their powers to create corporations." Harlan rejected the argument based on the reserve powers of the states on the grounds that such powers went counter to national supremacy in matters pertaining to the regulation of interstate commerce.

Holmes's lengthy dissenting statement, in which Chief Justice Fuller and Justices Peckham and White concurred, was a thorough canvass of the issues raised. Recognizing the importance of the suit, Holmes contended that "great cases like hard cases make bad law." He alluded to the "accident of immediate overwhelming interest which appeals to the feelings and distorts the judgment," and said he would have no part of it. The question before the Court, Holmes insisted, was whether the act of in-corporating the holding company was illegal under the Sherman law, and not whether it would end competition in a certain sec-tion of the country. Such a possible impact on trade was extrane-ous to the suit at hand. Furthermore, he objected to the "very sweeping and general character" of the working of the Sherman Act: "every contract, combination, or conspiracy"—this was the kind of overall proposition with which he was never comfortable. He judged that the effect which the Northern Securities Cor-poration might have on interstate commerce was at most indirect, in support of which he quoted approvingly from the majority opinion in the *E. C. Knight* case, regarded by reformers as an outrageous example of judicial blindness to the realities of monopoly. "Sticking to the exact words used in the Sherman Act," Holmes failed to see in the facts of the case any contract, combination or conspiracy in restraint of trade as these words were used in acceptable legal language. He appeared on less certain footing, however, when he proceeded to argue that a "single railroad down a narrow valley or through a mountain gorge monopolizes all the railroad transportation through that valley or gorge. Indeed, every railroad monopolizes in a popular sense the trade of some area." After this momentary lapse his line of reasoning strengthened, as he pointed out that somehow the notion was abroad that bigness in a monopoly translated ever and always into badness, a proposition not justified by the word-ing of the Sherman Act nor intellectually agreeable to Holmes. What is evident in this aspect of his dissent is a foreshadowing of the "rule of reason" which would color Court judgments of trust regulation in the next decade. In his dissent Holmes, true to habit, argued that "not every act done in furtherance of an unlawful end is an attempt or contrary to the law. There must be a certain nearness to the results. It is a question of proximity and degree...." No doubt Holmes had offered a respectable legal justification for his position. This did not enable him to escape the political fallout from the White House, however.[22]

V *Progressive Appearances*

Holmes's dissenting view in *Lochner* v. *New York*[23] (1905) and his majority opinion in *Swift and Company* v. *United States*[24] (1905), both of which followed closely on the heels of the *Northern Securities* case, served notice on Roosevelt, Lodge, or anyone else that he would be predictably unpredictable. The *Lochner* case had to do with the constitutionality of a New York state law which placed a limitation on the number of hours per day and per week a baker might be employed in a bakery. The state had exercised its police power in such a regulation, contending that maximum hours were related to the health of the bakers as well as of the consuming public. The law clashed immediately with the economic liberty of bakery owners to use their property in whatever manner they saw fit. The Supreme Court ruled against the state statute in a five-to-four decision. Mr. Justice Peckham, for the majority, found that the state had engaged in "meddlesome interference" with the right to purchase or sell labor as guaranteed by the due process clause of the Fourteenth Amendment, asserting that the law looked like regulation of hours for its own sake and had nothing to do with the health of the bakers involved. Holmes wrote a separate, dissenting judgment. It centered on five specific points: (1) the case was decided upon an economic theory which a large part of the country did not entertain; (2) it is settled that state laws may regulate life in many ways which we as legislators might think injudicious; (3) "General propositions do not decide case. The decision will depend on a judgment or intuition more subtle than any articulate major premise"; (4) the word "liberty" in the Fourteenth Amendment was perverted if it worked to obstruct the natural result, unless it can be said that a rational and fair person would admit, of necessity, that the law at issue would infringe fundamental principles; (5) "A reasonable man might think it [the New York law] a proper measure on the score of health." This dissenting opinion, containing as it did so much of the essence of Holmes's judicial thinking, has become a classic example of his legal philosophy.

Swift and Company v. *United States* marked another victory in the Roosevelt administration's attack on the trusts. Suitably enough, Holmes spoke for the majority in affirming the decree of a circuit court which had enjoined the meatpacking firm from engaging in unlawful restraints and monopolies. Swift and Company controlled over half of the whole trade and commerce in fresh meats among the states. The bill of particulars alleged against the company was impressive. It charged a combination of dealers in fresh meat throughout the country had agreed not to bid against each other in the livestock markets of the several states, to bid up prices for a few days to encourage cattlemen to send stock to the stock yards, to fix prices at which they would sell, to restrict shipments to maintain prices, to keep a blacklist of noncooperating dealers, to arrange rebates with railroads. The intent of all these activities, it was further charged, was "to monopolize and to prevent competition." Counsel for Swift answered that the charges did not set forth "sufficient definite or specific facts." Holmes's response for the Court showed his disposition to "nicely analyze" the legal problems in the case. He wrote in part; "The scheme is so vast that it presents a new problem in pleading. . . . Its size makes the violation of the law more conspicuous, and yet the same thing makes it impossible to fasten the principal fact to a certain time and place." Nonetheless Holmes concluded that "The scheme as a whole seems to us to be within reach of the law. The constituent elements are enough to give the scheme a body and, for all that we can say, to accomplish it. Moreover, whatever we may think of them separately when we take them up as distinct charges, they are alleged sufficiently as elements of the scheme." Beyond these considerations, Holmes also discerned from the facts in the case a clear illustration of "stream of commerce," one of the important derivative concepts of the commerce clause.

This argument in the *Swift* case in support of antitrust action was as thorough and as finely reasoned as was Holmes's dissent in the *Northern Securities* case, wherein he had reached an opposite conclusion. What may be said to account for his contrary interpretations in the two cases? Several different factors, especially if taken in combination, add up to an explanation. The physical evidence of the manipulation of prices by the Swift company agents is one such consideration. The tangible impact of combination is another. The vastness of the scheme itself, implying as it did a deliberate plan, seems also to have been persuasive. Finally, the very subject in the dispute—the shipment of food, a necessity of life—should be taken into account. If

Holmes was prepared to judge a case on its merits and not according to some generalized formula, the facts in *Swift and Company* v. *United States* were such as to convince him of the constitutionality of this particular regulation of a trust in the public interest.

VI *Dissenting Judge*

Holmes's predilection for dissent blossomed within three years of his coming on the Court. Whether or not his views laid down guidelines, marking out a future growth of the law, remained to be seen. Though reasonably sure that his interpretations were sound law, he did not insist on their dogmatic certainty. In *Missouri* v. *Illinois* (1905),[25] for example, he disagreed with the majority, which held that sewage entering the Mississippi River in Illinois made that state accountable for the evil effects of contaminated water downstream in Missouri. In a confrontation between two states, where the evidence presented by plaintiff and defendant appeared equally strong, Holmes declined to take sides. In *Haddock* v. *Haddock* (1905),[26] he dissented because he discerned further encroachments by the Court on state sovereignty in a suit involving divorce laws in New York and Connecticut. "I do not suppose that civilization will come to an end which ever way this case is decided," Holmes admitted, but he foresaw unnecessary mischief for innocent parties when state divorce laws were interfered with. Offering still another dissent in *Carroll* v. *Greenwich Insurance Company* (1905),[27] in which Holmes held constitutional an Iowa law which forbade fire-insurance companies doing business in the state from agreeing on rates, the need for judicial restraint came through as a paramount consideration in his reasoning. Holmes came to the defense of the eight-hour day for laborers and mechanics in a United States Navy shipyard in *Ellis* v. *United States* (1906).[28] The workmen party to the suit had been hired by a private contractor, a fact which the majority of the Court judged adequate reason to suspend the eight hour limitation on government employees. Such interpretations as the foregoing may be regarded as leading toward two of the more widely heralded of Holmes's dissents which hewed to the Progressive line: *Adair* v. *United*

States (1908)[29] and the *First Employers' Liability* cases (1908).[30] An examination of these cases and the Holmesian response to them may be especially helpful for seeing through to the center of his impulse to dissent. Whether or not his departure from the Court majority made Holmes a judicial prophet, no one could say at the time.

Adair v. *United States* involved the so-called "yellow-dog" provision of the Erdman Act of 1898. This was a broad, regulatory law respecting railroad labor policy. Section 10 of the act specifically made illegal any labor contract part of which included a promise not to join a union upon employment. Discrimination against workers who were union members was also prohibited. The Court held Section 10 of the Erdman Act unconstitutional. Speaking for the majority, Justice Harlan held the provision an unreasonable interference with freedom of contract, a denial of the economic liberty protected against congressional action by the due-process clause of the Fifth Amendment. Referring particularly to the *Lochner* case, Harlan concluded that the statute was the kind "no government can legally justify in a free land." Holmes thought otherwise, offering his interpretation in phrases notable for clarity and candor:

The ground on which this particular law is held bad is not so much that it deals with matters remote from commerce among the States as that it interferes with the paramount individual rights secured by the Fifth Amendment. . . . I confess that I think that the right to make contracts at will that has been derived from the word liberty in the Amendments has been stretched to its extreme by the decision. . . . Where there is, or generally is believed to be, an important ground of public policy for restraint, the Constitution does not forbid it, whether this Court agrees or disagrees with the policy pursued.

In the *Adair* opinion Holmes's argument was mainly "legalistic." His dissent in the *First Employer's Liability Cases* made use of a different approach. In 1906 Congress passed an Employers' Liability Act, which stated that every common carrier engaged in commerce in the District of Columbia or in any territory or between the states or with foreign nations was liable to its employees for damages attributable to injury or death because of the negligence of management or other employees or from material defects in tools and equipment which workers were required to use. This law in effect abrogated the old common law "fellow-servant" rule, under which an employer could not be held responsible for injuries which might be sustained by a worker on the job. Upon the accidental death of two railroad men soon after the enactment of the statute, the railroads involved brought suit, denying the authority of the Congress to legislate for "every common carrier." The Supreme Court ruled the act bad law because no distinction was drawn between intrastate and interstate carriers. This was held to amount to an invasion of the police powers of the states appropriate to intrastate commerce. While agreeing that Congress had authority to regulate employers' liability in interstate traffic, the law as written was struck down. Holmes's willingness to depart from the majority position was especially arresting, inasmuch as he chose to construe the phraseology of the act loosely, perhaps because of the nature of the facts of the suit. His brief rejoinder to the court speaks for itself:

I must admit that I think there are strong reasons in favor of the statute adopted by a majority of the Court. But as it is possible to read words in such a way as to save the constitutionality of the Act, I think they should be taken in that narrow sense. The phrase "every common carrier engaged in trade or commerce" may be construed to mean "while engaged in trade or commerce" without violence to the habits of English speech, and to govern all that follows.

Congress acted quickly to meet the objections stated in the majority opinion, passing new legislation in 1908. In 1912 in the *Second Employers' Liability Cases* the Supreme Court unanimously declared the new act constitutional. But it was not until a major overhaul of labor law, the Norris-LaGuardia Act of 1931, that the yellow-dog contract was prohibited, by which time Holmes had left the bench.

VII *Patterns*

After six years on the Supreme Court, the pattern of Holmes's interpretations of the law was established for the next ten. Ever the independent judge, he came down on the side of increasing federal regulations in the public interest. His attitude toward a 1907 congressional law making it a punishable offense to keep alien women for purposes of prostitution within three years of entry into the country was an example. In *Keller* v. *United States* (1909),[31] he dissented from a majority opinion which overturned the law on the grounds that it invaded the reserve powers of the states. As Holmes counter-argued: "If a woman were found living in a house of prostitution within a week of her arrival, no one, I suppose, would doubt that it tended to show she was in the business when she arrived. But how far back such an inference will reach is a matter of degree, like most questions of life. And, while a period of three years may seem too long, I am not prepared to say, against the judgment of the Congress, that it is too long." Holmes was convinced that such a regulation was in the best interests of the community and should therefore be sustained by the court. When the Mann Act of 1910, aimed at the white-slave traffic, came before the court in *Hoke* v. *United States* (1913), he had no difficulty in agreeing with the unanimous decision of the Court, written by Justice McKenna, who asserted that "the powers reserved to the states and those conferred on the nation are adapted to the exercise, whether independently or concurrently, to promote the general welfare, material and moral."[32]

Yet Holmes remained enough of his own man to fire off dissents when he found Congress or the Court exceeding their powers at the expense of the states. In *Pullman* v. *Kansas* (1909),[33] the Court held that a Kansas statute requiring that railroads operating within its jurisdiction pay a percentage fee levied on capitalizing was bad law. Justice Harlan for the majority decreed such a fee an unconstitutional burden on interstate commerce. Holmes thought otherwise in an opinion in which he was joined by Chief Justice Fuller in dissent. Seeking to "add a few words on the broad proposition put forward that the Constitution forbids the charge" exacted by the state, he took exception to the maxim of Marshall that the power to tax is the power to destroy. Such a tax was not of necessity an interference with interstate commerce if it did no more than subject that commerce to the same regulation as imposed on local business. In another case Holmes offered a defense of state

Court decisions in *Kuhn* v. *Fairmont Coal Company* (1909).[34] At issue was a West Virginia Supreme Court ruling which held that a coal company was not obliged to leave enough coal in the mines to support the earth above. The majority ruled that the circuit court of appeals was not bound by the state court precedent. Holmes disagreed; in his view, laws governing real estate depend on statutes and rulings of state agencies; it was not the business of the federal courts to find arbitrary exceptions. As the facts involved conditions by nature and necessity "peculiarly local," federal interference was hardly justified. An overview of Holmes's positions in cases great and small attests to his endorsement of liberal nationalism—whatever his intention—modified by his habit of judging every case on its own merits.

The pattern of Holmes's judicial thinking was well established by 1908, but a number of cases after that time further illustrate the play of his mind, irrespective of the concurring or dissenting character of opinions. While he voted with the majority in *Interstate Commerce Commission* v. *Illinois Central Railroad Company* (1910), which sustained the narrow review principle of the Hepburn Act, he joined Chief Justice White in dissenting in *Interstate Commerce Commission* v. *Chicago, Rock Island, and Pacific Railroad Company* (1910), siding with White against the majority because of the "idiosyncrasies of this particular case." However, in the great regulating decisions of 1911, *Standard Oil Company* v. *United States, United States* v. *American Tobacco Company,* and *Hipolite Egg Company* v. *United States* —the latter case sustained the Pure Food and Drug Act—Holmes consistently stood with the majority, endorsing regulation of corporations in the public interest. But two years later, in *United States* v. *Winslow,*[35] he wrote a majority opinion which refused to authorize the break-up of the United Shoe Machinery Company under the Sherman Act. "On the face of it," he wrote, "the combination was simply an effort after greater efficiency." The company in question had not necessarily violated existing antitrust statutes. Consistent with the foregoing view was Holmes's dissent in *Dr. Miles Medical Company* v. *Park & Sons Company* (1911),[36] in which he spoke of "superstitions" surrounding restraint of trade between the states. "I think that, at least, it is

safe to say the most enlightened judicial policy is to let people
manage their own business in their own way, unless the ground
for interference is very clear." Holmes argued further that while
it may be prudent to have controls on interstate traffic of necessities, he failed to see how Dr. Miles Medicine fit into such a
category. "To let people manage their own business" had a
singular Yankee ring about it. But in fact he was combining
inherited instincts with an understanding of the law in the *Dr.
Miles* case, as he also did in *Noble State Bank* v. *Haskell*
(1911),[37] wherein he cautioned "about pressing the broad words
of the Fourteenth Amendment to a drily logical extreme. . . .
We have few scientifically certain criteria for legislation," he
went on, "and as it often is difficult to mark the line where what
is called police power by the States is limited by the Constitution of the United States, judges should be slow to read into
the latter a *nolumus mutare* [we oppose change] as against the
law-making power."

The intensification of Progressivism from 1912 onward meant
that increasing numbers of cases before the court concerned
issues stemming from the wave of reform legislation. Holmes,
however, continued to follow his basic judicial philosophy with
little or no discernible concession to the Progressive mood. In
Cedar Rapids Gas Company v. *Cedar Rapids* (1912),[38] for
example, he held that the utility company in question was
properly regulated by an agreement which discounted the price
of gas supplied to customers upon early payment of bills. Cedar
Rapids Gas Company claimed that such a regulation amounted
to a violation of the Fourteenth Amendment. Holmes, for the
majority, argued that such a regulation was reasonable enough.
"An adjustment of this sort under a power to regulate rates has
to steer between Scylla and Charybdis," he observed. "On the
one side if the franchise is taken to mean that the most profit-
able return that could be got, free from competition, is protected by the Fourteenth Amendment, then the power to regulate
is null. On the other hand if the power to regulate withdraws
the protection of the Amendment altogether, then the property
is nought. This is not a matter of economic theory, but a fair
interpretation of a bargain." Holmes's line of reasoning was not

much else than common sense applied to the law. Similarly, he agreed with a majority court stand in favor of state regulation of rail rates in the *Minnesota Rate* cases (1914), confirming the rate making power of the Interstate Commerce Commission. Holmes also believed it constitutional to institute criminal proceedings under the Sherman Act. He challenged the idea of "malice" as an essential ingredient incident to prosecution, carrying a majority of the Court with him in *Nash* v. *United States* (1913).[39] On the other hand, in *International Harvester Company* v. *Kentucky* (1914)[40]—and in an opinion he was at pains to insist was consistent with the *Nash* ruling—he found that the company had not violated state law when, under Kentucky statutes, producers of grain, tobacco, and other farm products raised in the state were allowed to combine in order to improve price prospects. Given the facts of the case (tobacco growers had trebled their prices by means of combinations, whereas International Harvester had raised its prices by 10 to 15 percent), as well as the law itself (discrimination, by implication at least), Holmes set down a majority opinion in favor of the plaintiff. In the sphere of trade-union activities he wrote the majority view in *Gompers* v. *United States* (1914),[41] which justified contempt proceedings against a union leader who defied court injunctions. And in *Lawlor* v. *Loewe* (1914),[42] Holmes dissented from the majority of the Court, which exonerated the United Hatters of North America from the charge of conspiring to restrain trade in interstate commerce by recourse to a boycott. "It is a tax on credulity," he said, "to ask any one to believe that members of labor unions at that time did not know that the primary and secondary boycott . . . were means expected to be employed in the effort to unionize shops." Holmes did not always follow where Progressivism might lead.

VIII   *Holmes and Brandeis*

When in 1916 Holmes was joined on the Supreme Court by Louis D. Brandeis, he was welcoming an old and trusted friend as well as a judicial mind much in sympathy with his own. At the time of his appointment, Brandeis noted that his views in regard to the Constitution were "very much those of Mr. Justice Holmes."[43] The two men had first met in 1879 when they were practicing attorneys in Boston. Not only did Brandeis gain intellectual stimulation from the friendship, but he enjoyed the society of Wendell and Fanny Holmes as well. A weekend invitation to Mattapoisett was followed by occasional dinners at the Parker House, where the Holmeses usually dined. Brandeis was interested in what his friend had to say in his Lowell Lectures, and attended at least one lecture during the series. He was also instrumental in persuading William Weld to establish the Weld Professorship at the Harvard Law School in 1882, to which Holmes was named. When shortly thereafter Holmes moved to the Massachusetts bench, Brandeis wrote him: "As one of the bar I rejoice. As part of the Law School I mourn. As your friend I congratulate you."[45] Though their careers diverged somewhat thereafter, the friendship remained unimpaired. Brandeis spoke prophetically of "the deep impression" which Holmes would make "upon Federal jurisprudence" on his appointment to the Supreme Court.[46] In 1909, with the case of *Muller* v. *Oregon* before the high court—the case in which Brandeis launched the sociological brief—Holmes was glad enough to join the majority in upholding the state law of Oregon which placed restrictions on hours which women might be employed in industry. But Holmes and Brandeis had distinctly different approaches to the law, despite a definite intellectual kinship. "Brandeis had an insatiable appetite for fact and ... I hate them except as pegs for generalizations, but I admire the gift and wish I had a barn which I could store them for use at need," Holmes once admitted to Harold Laski.[47] More importantly, he found "great comfort in his [Brandeis] companionship."[48] It seemed to be poetic justice laced with irony that as Holmes was growing older in his unintentional stand for liberalism he was joined by the younger, more vigorous, and deliberately liberal Brandeis. While he did not always understand the data Brandeis put forth in his opinions, in a sense a new era had commenced on the Supreme Court, best summed up in the phrase soon to be made familiar: "Holmes and Brandeis dissenting."

One such dissent, typical of an almost instinctive brotherhood enjoyed by Holmes and Brandeis, came in *Southern Pacific Company* v. *Jensen* (1916),[49] a suit brought to challenge a New York Workmen's Compensation Law. In unloading timber from a ship that had come to New York from Galveston, a stevedore had broken his neck and died. Under the law an award was made to the man's family, but the award was contested on the grounds that the statute interfered with commerce between the states and was a violation of the due process clause. Holmes argued that it was "established" that the state had the constitutional power to pass laws giving rights and imposing liabilities for acts done upon the high seas, when there had been no such rights or liabilities before. Consequently, he concluded there was nothing to hinder the state from so doing in the case of a maritime tort. As maritime law was not a *corpus juris* but "a very limited body of customs and ordinances of the sea," the worker was justified in having some recourse at law. "The mere silence of Congress [did not] exclude the statute or common law of a state from supplementing the wholly inadequate maritime law of the time of the constitution in the regulation of personal rights...."

Holmes and Brandeis also dissented, memorably, in *Hammer* v. *Dagenhart* (1918), with Holmes writing the opinion, joined by Justices Clarke and McKenna, in what proved to be a five-to-four decision. The Keating-Owens Child Labor Act of 1916 was the law at issue, a congressional statute prohibiting the shipment in interstate commerce of goods produced in factories where child labor was employed. In Holmes's opinion it was beyond dispute that the statute was within the power of the Congress to pass, that the power to regulate included the power to prohibit, that it mattered not that a supposed evil preceded or followed the transportation of goods in interstate commerce, and that the act did not meddle with anything belonging to the states. Despite the presence of Brandeis on the Court and the persistence of Holmes, who was so often supported by McKenna, liberal nationalism had met with a setback, the Court striking down the federal child labor law. But it was really a matter of ups and downs: The *Dagenhart* defeat pairs with *Wilson* v. *New* (1917),[50] a case in which Holmes, Brandeis, and McKenna formed part of the majority, declaring constitutional the Adamson Eight Hour Act, limiting the hours of railway workers on interstate trains.

IX *"Natural Law" Restated*

Decisions of the High Court apart, Holmes's theory of law, its
origins and its essence, received an unambiguous if somewhat
negative statement in his essay, "Natural Law," which appeared
at this time. In it he again directly challenged those who continued to hold the law as an absolute, having its source in either
God or the State or the inalienable rights of man. Decrying man's
tendency to demand the superlative, which he thought well
illustrated in the "jurist's search for criteria of universal validity,"
Holmes invoked the standard of force. Truth "was the majority
vote of that nation which can lick all others." Putting the same
basic idea more adroitly, he spoke of truth as "the system of my
intellectual limitations," that is, what he and the majority of his
fellow human beings could not help but believe. Admitting that
deep seated prejudices can not be argued about Holmes noted
that different men adhere to different prejudices; and, he continued, if these "prejudices are sufficiently far reaching we try to
kill the other man rather than let him have his way." Truth in
some fixed form, in other words, whether in life or in the law did
not exist, and judges who sought it or claimed to have found it
he dismissed as naive. Holmes fortified his position by arguing
that "I do not see any rational ground for demanding the
superlative—for being dissatisfied unless we are assured that our
truth is cosmic truth . . . that the ultimates of a little creature on
this little earth are the last word of the unimaginable whole."
Instead, he concluded, "it is enough for us that the universe has
produced us and has within it, as less than it, all that we believe
and love." "Natural Law," blunt in its message, was a powerful
essay, despite the negative inflections. Holmes was once again the
acknowledged spokesman of a philosophy of legal realism which
had cut itself loose from the old moral moorings. Critics of
legal realism complained that Holmes and the like-minded were
adrift. Holmes saw it another way. "Philosophy does not furnish
motives," he wrote in "Natural Law," "but it shows men that
they are not fools for doing what they already want to do."
For scientific man in the twentieth century, principle followed
action rather than action following principle. This was a general
rule of life to which the law was no exception.[51]

X   *His Own Man*

By 1917 Oliver Wendell Holmes had been fifteen years on the Supreme Court, with another fifteen still to serve. Not yet a legend, he had won the enduring respect of his peers. Such appreciations were based, in part, on his scholar's approach to the law. Indeed, his place became known as the scholar's seat, afterwards to be occupied by Cardozo and Frankfurter. Holmes had displayed a penetrating knowledge of the law, erudite yet in touch with social reality. He had also developed into something of a loner on the bench, content to side with conservatives or liberals, depending on the facts of the case, the law, or the constitutional provision at issue. Such an assessment is consistent with the notion of Holmes as the creator of a "new jurisprudence based on assumption which flatly contradicted some of the basic assumptions of time-honored jurisprudence." To Jerome Frank, for example, Holmes harbored revolutionary ideas which were little heeded for years but which led directly to the rise of legal realism. While there was much in the first half of his tenure on the Supreme Court to support Roscoe Pound's claim that Holmes "knew when value judgments drawn from outside of the body of authoritarian legal materials were in order," his frequent attacks on general rules and moral elements were clearly major features of his legal philosophy. Frank makes claims for Holmes as a legal realist which are perhaps too exclusive; Pound insists upon a moral element which is not consistently present. Such rival interpretations of Holmes's legal philosophy tend to reaffirm the image of Holmes as "his own man."[52]

CHAPTER 6

War and Normalcy: Judgments

I World War

WHEN hostilities broke out in Europe in 1914, Oliver Wendell Holmes was profoundly disturbed at the prospect of a world at war. His immediate sympathies were with England, hardly surprising given his background of study and his circle of English friends. He wrote Sir Frederick Pollock in September: "I, like the rest of us, prayed for your success against this march of Tamerlane. . . . There is no use talking about it, but my heart aches with you all."[1] In those first days of the conflict, the enormity of the tragedy of the Great War was beyond the perceptions of most men, as patriotic people everywhere and of whatever class rallied behind their nations. Holmes, the American, tried to be detached, confessing that "in truth I should grieve only less to have German than to have English civilization broken up or hampered."[2] Even with the fighting and dying so far away, however, he found such a posture difficult. In October 1914, he told the American diplomat Lewis Einstein, "I believe in 'my country right or wrong,' and next to my country my crowd, and England is my crowd. I earnestly long to see her keep on top, and yet I shall grieve if, as I hope, Germany is crushed." And he continued: "I suppose the war was inevitable, and yet whatever the event, it fills me with sorrow, disinterested sorrow, apart from its effects upon us and from my personal sympathy with England."[3] The American Civil War had had a shaping effect on Oliver Wendell Holmes, and although that had been decades before, he felt a real kinship with the men in the trenches.[4] Was this vicarious experience of World War I not a reminder of how his own ordeal by fire had hardened his outlook on life? When the war spread and the United States joined the conflict in the spring of 1917, a commitment to a

116

British triumph wedded with his own patriotic impulses.[5] Perhaps it was partially the impact of the war, once it had become America's fight, which imparted to his judicial viewpoints thereafter· their quality of judgments—as distinct from interpretations—of the law. Both the world and the nation appeared no longer able to indulge the luxury of anything less than clearcut responses to the great issues arising from Armageddon. Doomsday—or its individual equivalent, death—seemed to stand too close to admit of ambiguous answers. Differences of opinion grew more stark in their reality, war had worked to reduce beliefs to a jarring simplicity. Judicial decisions now deserved a stand well taken, rather than theories finely spun. Or was Time finally forcing Holmes to think absolutely about Truth? Did the war in combination with his own advancing years paint him into a philosophical corner at last? As useful as such consideration may be for explaining the presence of a new vein of iron in an old judge's pronouncements, part of the answer may well lie elsewhere. Had Oliver Wendell Holmes begun to believe what an increasing number of people were saying: that he was one of the wisemen of the tribe and deserved to be listened to, especially in a time of crisis? Admitting that his "detachment and would-be impartiality" were "somewhat shaken" and that he would do what he could "to cherish in my countrymen an unphilosophic hatred of Germany and German ways,"[6] he was not unmindful of the veneration accorded him by many of the brightest young men in Washington during the war years.[7] And if Truth came down to no more than things as they were, then it behooved Mr. Justice Holmes to tell it straight. Whatever the explanation, Holmes emerged over the last fifteen years of his justiceship as more the judge, and, accordingly, less the legal theorist. His decisions, whether in agreement with the Court or offered in dissent, had an unmistakable cut and thrust about them.

Woodrow Wilson worried aloud of the terrible thing it would be to lead the American people into war. The kind of massive reorganization of government necessary to bring the full weight of the nation to bear on events posed new and troublesome constitutional questions, from the conscription of millions of men to the direct entrance by the federal government into economic enterprises long held to be the peculiar preserves of the business community. Under grants of power delegated him by the Congress as well as due to an accretion of authority arising from the crisis itself, President Wilson became a virtual dictator for the duration of the war. Even more disturbing was the mental and emotional conformity required of the people of the United States. Constitutional guarantees of civil and political rights were challenged, modified, and—in the thinking of many—disregarded altogether. Such were the demands of total war in the twentieth century.

II *The Court Responds*

The Supreme Court had no difficulty in declaring the Selective Service Act constitutional in the *Selective Draft Law Cases* (1918), nor the Army Appropriation Act which authorized presidential seizure and operation of the railroads (*Northern Pacific Railroad Company* v. *North Dakota*, 1919). In each instance the vote of the justices was unanimously in favor of the power of the sovereign state. When it came to the war and the Bill of Rights, however, the unity of the Court was eventually shattered. At issue was the constitutionality of two measures, the Espionage Act of 1917 and the Espionage Act of 1918, the latter commonly referred to as the Sedition Act. The 1917 law, which guarded against efforts to disrupt the armed forces of the United States either in the process of recruitment or in military operations, came to the test in *Schenck* v. *United States* (1919). Schenck was accused of attempting to bring about insubordination in the ranks of the armed forces by causing to have mailed to individuals who had been called up under the draft a document designed to incite disobedience to the law. He was charged further with using the mails to transmit his plea, sending material which the law declared was unmailable. As general secretary of the Socialist party, Schenck personally supervised the printing and distribution of 15,000 pieces of mail to inductees. The gist of his defense was that the Selective Service Act contravened the first section of the Thirteenth Amendment, which protected against involuntary servitude. Holmes delivered the unanimous judgment of the Court, which found Schenck guilty and the Selective Service law constitutional. The essence of his argument can be reduced to a few sentences.

We admit that in many places and in ordinary times the defendants in saying all that was said in the circular would have been within their constitutional rights. But the character of every act depends upon circumstances in which it is done. . . . The most stringent protection of free speech would not protect a man in falsely shouting fire in a theater and causing a panic. It does not even protect a man from an injunction against uttering words that may have all the effect of force. . . . The question in every case is whether the words used are used in such circumstances and are of such a nature as to create a clear and present danger that they will bring about the substantive evils that Congress has a right to prevent. It is a question of proximity and degree.

When a nation is at war many things that might be said in time of peace are such a hindrance to its effort that their utterance will not be endured so long as men fight and then no court would regard them as protected by any constitutional right. It seems admitted that if an actual obstruction of the recruiting of service were proved, liability for words that produced that effect might be enforced.[8]

The "clear and present danger" rule which Holmes had enunciated and by which the *Schenck* case became distinguished was akin to the "rule of proximate causation" found in the common law both of England and America. The finality of Holmes's judgment in the case is better appreciated from his remarks to Laski, written the day the *Schenck* decision was handed down. " . . . [The] real substance [of the case] being: "Damn your eyes —that's the way it's going to be."[9] In wars, Holmes was saying, there were only friends or enemies, the finer shadings of the law lost temporarily in the blinding flash of passions.

Holmes wrote two other majority opinions at this time which tended to show that the power of the sovereign state, when confronted by the rights of its citizens, must prevail. A certain Frohwerk appealed to the Supreme Court to reverse a lower court decision which declared him guilty of violating the Espionage Act of 1917 by reason of his publication of a newspaper, the *Missouri Staats Zeitung*. His appeal was based especially on the guarantees provided him by the First Amendment. In reply for the Court Holmes answered in part that "to that argument we think it necessary to add what has been said in *Schenck* v. *United States*, only that the First Amendment, while prohibiting legislation against free speech as such, can not have been, and obviously was not, intended to give immunity for every possible use of language. . . . We venture to believe that neither Hamilton nor Madison, nor any other competent person then or later, ever supposed that to make criminal the counselling of a murder within the jurisdiction of Congress would be unconstitutional interference with free speech." The motivation of Frohwerk in seeking to discourage the American war effort was nationalistic —his newspaper spoke of the "unconquerable spirit and the undiminished strength of the German nation"—but motivations were irrelevant to the operation of the law and thus to the judgments set down by Holmes.[10] The other case, consistent with the *Schenck* and *Frohwerk* judgments, was that of *Debs* v. *United States* (1919). The protests of Debs against the war were based on a mixture of socialism and pacifism. Holmes's majority opinion simply cited the *Schenck* case and its reasoning.[11] As he confided to Laski, "in the only question before us I could not doubt about the law." At the same time he admitted that he "greatly regretted having to write" the *Debs* ruling, expressing doubts about the wisdom of the government in pressing either the Frohwerk or the Debs indictments: "Of course I know that donkeys and knaves would represent us as concurring in the condemnation of Debs because he was a dangerous agitator. Of course too, as far as that is concerned, he [Debs] might split his guts without my interfering with him or sanctioning interference."[12] Such private thoughts, though intimating a possible alteration of views on the issue of constitutional guarantees under the First Amendment, were insufficient to persuade Holmes to abandon the letter of the law.

But he was about to alter his judgment. The Sedition Act of 1918 provided for far more sweeping restrictions on freedom of speech than had the earlier law, under which all the foregoing cases had been argued. So extreme were these limitations on free speech that Holmes and Brandeis were quick to utter doubts about its application. The key was *Abrams* v. *United States* (1919). In the long view it proved also to be a pivotal case in Holmes's thinking about First Amendment guarantees. Throughout the 1920s in a series of suits, Holmes and Brandeis dissented from the majority, registering their belief in individual freedoms, the initial expression of which came in the *Abrams* case.

Abrams and his cohorts had printed and scattered from rooftops a few thousand leaflets protesting the dispatch of American troops to Russia at the time of the Bolshevik Revolution. A majority of the Court chose to uphold a lower court conviction of the individuals in question, whereupon Abrams appealed to the Supreme Court for a reversal of judgment on the grounds that his First Amendment freedoms had been denied. The Court, speaking through Justice Clarke, deemed the evidence ample that Abrams had sought to obstruct the American war effort in a manner that violated the Espionage (Sedition) Act of 1918. The rule applied was that of "bad tendency," a less stringent test than "clear and present danger" and thus a stricter limitation of freedom of expression. Holmes demurred. Having given the Court's ruling in the *Schenck, Frohwerk,* and *Debs* cases, "I thought it proper to state what I thought the limits of the doctrine," as he explained to Pollock.[13] He objected in the first place to the evidence, declaring the message of the leaflets too vague and in fact too silly to be a distraction from the war effort. It was not enough that the actions of the accused had created a "bad tendency." Proof was needed that the leaflets had created a "clear and present danger" since the punishment meted out, twenty years in prison, spoke the dimension of the crime. And yet there was much more to Holmes's dissent than reservations about the evidence. He observed that he believed the defendant had as much right to publish what he had, as the government had to publish the Constitution "now vainly invoked" by him. Holmes then gave voice to the central proposition of what may be termed a liberal rendering of the Bill of Rights:

Persecution for the expression of opinions seems to me perfectly logical. If you have no doubt of your premises or your power and want a certain result with all your heart you naturally express your wishes in law and sweep away all opposition. To allow opposition by speech seems to indicate that you think the speech impotent, as when a man says that he has squared the circle, or that you do not care wholeheartedly for the result, or that you doubt either your power or your premises. But when men have realized that time has upset many fighting faiths, they may come to believe even more than they believe the very foundations of their conduct that the ultimate good desired is better reached by free trade in ideas,—that the best test of truth is the power of the thought to get itself accepted in the competition of the market; and that truth is the only ground upon which their wishes can be carried out. That, at any rate, is the theory of our Constitution. It is an experiment, as all life is an experiment. Every year, if not every day, we have to wager our salvation upon some prophecy based upon imperfect knowledge. While that experiment is part of our system I think that we should be eternally vigilant against attempts to check the expression of opinions that we loathe and believe to be fraught with death, unless they so imminently threaten immediate interference with the lawful and pressing purpose of the law that an immediate check is required to save the country.[14]

Such is the stuff of which judgments are made. Nor is the impact of this eloquent statement weakened by Holmes's private remark that he took "the extremist view in favor of free speech, (in which, in the abstract, I have no very enthusiastic belief, though I hope I would die for it). . . ."[15] To note that Holmes had become more judgmental and less interpretative underscores the paradoxes of his thought: his confessed lack of enthusiasm, be it remembered, was for an abstraction; but his hope of dying in defense of free speech, were it to come about, would be a hard fact. Holmes believed above all in hard facts: that which "he could not help but believe" was for him true. In this subtle yet obvious way, he came to grips with the right of free speech and other personal liberties, and in the last dozen years or so of his justiceship judged cases accordingly.[16]

III Civil Libertarian

The Abrams dissent made Oliver Wendell Holmes a civil libertarian willy-nilly. As history can become what people believe to have been so, rather than what in fact was so, in such a fashion Holmes earned his name as a defender of the moral rights of individual citizens against the power of government. Such a state of affairs was not unlike his reputation as a Progressive judge where intent and motivation became obscured by developments of a much larger kind than the law itself. What

Holmes believed he was doing in defending civil liberties was simply applying the law. Not that he lacked a certain sympathy for the individuals involved in the cases which came before the Court. The evidence shows, however, that he based his judgments not on an abstract theory of rights but upon social circumstances in which men happened to find themselves at a given time. Beyond this was Holmes's highly personalized commitment to acceptance or rejection of rights in fact and rights in the abstract. It must always be kept in mind that for Holmes a right started from his definition of law "as a statement of the circumstances in which public force will be brought to bear upon men through courts."[17] If some preferred to read a moral element into Holmes's opinions in the civil liberty cases, he could do little, though he might protest that "I think our morally tinted words have caused a great deal of confused thinking about rights."[18] In *American Bank and Trust Company* v. *Federal Bank* (1912), he had noted that "the word 'right' is one of the most deceptive of pit-falls; it is so easy to step from a qualified meaning in the premise to an unqualified one in the conclusion. Most rights are qualified."[19] Those who seconded Holmes's judgments frequently ignored the "pit-falls" of which they had been warned. Such words as rights were "a constant solicitation to fallacy."[20] The warnings had been sounded clearly for those who would listen.

As late as 1920 the Supreme Court continued to have under consideration cases involving freedom of the press arising from World War I restrictions. One such suit, in which Holmes and Brandeis dissented, was *Milwaukee Socialist Democratic Publishing Company* v. *Burleson* (1920). As postmaster general, Burleson had denied access to the mails to the *Milwaukee Leader*, a newspaper edited by Victor Berger which had actively opposed America's part in the war. The crux of the case was Burleson's exercise of judgment, acting in Brandeis's phrase, as "a universal censor." But under the Espionage Act of 1917, the Court believed that such a use of power was legitimate. In Justice Clarke's words: "The Constitution was adopted to preserve our Government, not to serve as a protecting screen for those who while claiming its privileges, seek to destroy it." Holmes and Brandeis gave separate dissenting opinions. In part Holmes wrote:

The United States may give up the Post Office when it sees fit, but while it carries it on, the use of the mails is almost as much a part of free speech as the right to use our tongues and it would take very strong language to convince me that the Congress ever intended to give such a practically despotic power to any one man. There is no pretense that it has done so.[21]

In a similar case the next year, *Leach v. Carlile Postmaster* (1921), wherein the Post Office refused to transmit advertising literature for "Organo Tablets" on the grounds of fraudulent representation of medicine, Holmes and Brandeis again refused to concur in the majority opinion. Holmes stated his position forcefully:

I do not suppose that any one would say that the freedom of written speech is less protected by the First Amendment than the freedom of the spoken word. Therefore I can not understand by what authority Congress undertakes to authorize anyone to determine in advance, on the grounds before us, that certain words shall not be uttered. Even those who interpret the Amendment most strictly agree that it was intended to prevent previous restraint.[22]

For Holmes, at least, the basis of the judgment was what the law would allow as distinct from the abstract rights of citizens.

Constitutional guarantees of individual liberties might and did include matters other than freedom of speech of the press. Holmes wrote a particularly outspoken majority opinion in *Silverthorne Lumber Company v. United States* (1921), a case in which a federal district attorney, "without a shadow of authority," seized papers and documents from a company office while gathering evidence in a suit pending against the company. Frederick W. Silverthorne had refused to obey a court order to yield the papers, in response to which the district attorney moved in without benefit of warrants. Based on the information thus secured, new indictments were framed by government attorneys. Holmes's opinion lashed out at the officials involved: "it must be assumed that the Government planned or at all events ratified the whole performance." He spoke harshly of the government's intention to use illegally acquired data to support indictments: "the proposition could not be presented more nakedly." He dismissed government regrets over the incident as insincere: the constitution covered not only physical possession but the knowledge gained from that possession. Otherwise, Holmes concluded, the Fourth Amendment is reduced to "a form of words."[23] In a somewhat later case, *United States* v. *Sullivan* (1927), the defendant refused to indicate in his federal income tax return the source of certain sums of money derived, it was alleged, from activities in violation of the Eighteenth Amendment. The defendant's reason for refusing to disclose the information stemmed from the protection against self-incrimination guaranteed in the Fifth Amendment. But Holmes, for the Court, was of the "opinion that the protection of the Fifth Amendment was pressed too far." He also stated that "it would be an extreme if not an extravagant application of the Fifth Amendment to say that it authorized a man to refuse to state the amount of his income because it had been made in crime."[24] The *Silverthorne* and *Sullivan* cases were basic reminders by Holmes of the limits placed by the Constitution on both the government and its citizens.

Holmes's reputation as a civil libertarian was greatly advanced by three well-known dissents in *Gitlow* v. *New York* (1924), *Olmstead* v. *United States* (1927), and *United States* v. *Schwimmer* (1928). In each instance he and Brandeis stood together against majority opinion, adding substantially to the meaning of "Holmes and Brandeis dissenting." A look at the facts and judgments in each of these cases shows how much his position was a Holmesian mixture of law and morality—though in the *Schwimmer* opinion personal tastes momentarily may have secured an upper hand.

Under a New York law Gitlow had been found guilty of advocating criminal anarchy. Typical of his appeals advocating an overthrow of the government was "The Left Wing Manifesto," a document representing the extreme left-wing position of the Socialist party, preaching class struggle, industrial strikes, and open revolt leading to the dictatorship of the proletariat. All this the Supreme Court declared was no mere abstraction but "the language of direct incitement," not protected by the Fourteenth Amendment. Holmes, however, insisted that the liberty guaranteed against state interference by the due process clause of the amendment did indeed cover the publications submitted as evidence by the government. He cited the "clear and present danger" rule from the *Schenck* case and explicitly rejected the "bad tendency" principle of *Abrams* v. *United States.* As to the facts, he found in them "no present danger of an attempt to overthrow the Government by force." Allowing himself the luxury of some philosophizing—"every idea is an incitement"—nevertheless the law was the wellspring of Holmes's dissent.[25] "I let out a page of slack on the rights of an ass to drool about proletarian dictatorship," he wrote Laski. "Free speech means to most people, you may say anything that I don't think shocking."[26] There were no absolutes, in other words, beyond "the dominant force of the community."[27]

A citizen's protection against government wire-tapping done to gain evidence in a conviction for criminal activity came before the Court in *Olmstead* v. *United States.* This case dealt with individuals accused of transporting intoxicating beverages in interstate commerce as proscribed by the Volstead Act. The constitutional issues involved both the Fourth Amendment, securing persons against trespass, and the Fifth Amendment, protecting against self-incrimination. A majority of the justices were satisfied that wire-tapping did not violate the guarantees of either amendment, given the particulars of this case. Chief Justice Taft, for the Court, asserted that there had been no search, no seizure, and no entry. He went on to point out that only the sense of hearing had been employed and that furthermore the actions of the government officers took place away from the premises of the plaintiff. Trespass therefore had not occurred. While Brandeis made an exhaustive case for freedom from wire-tap by public officials, Holmes was content to "add but a few words." Those "few words" were to leave some memorable echoes: "for my part I think it a less evil that some criminals should escape than that the Government should play an ignoble part."[28] There being no body of precedents by which the Court was bound, as Holmes admitted, it can be assumed that for him wire-tapping was governed by his "can't help" rubric. Wire-tapping by the government was judged to be wrong because he could not help but believe that it was wrong. Viewed in this light, Holmes's "can't helps" come pretty close to "self-evident truths," with the definite coloration of morality which that phrase implies and which he had steadfastly rejected. There is some justification, in consequence, for imputing to Holmes a morality in this judgment of the law. Delicate is the distinction between "can't help" and conscience.

The confrontation of Court ruling and personal predilection was one feature of the *Rosika Schwimmer* case in 1928. Schwimmer had been denied citizenship because she had stated in her application that she could not in conscience take up arms in defense of the nation. The Naturalization Act of 1906 required applicants to be willing to swear to "support and defend the Constitution and the laws of the United States against all enemies" and otherwise to show attachment to the principles of the Constitution. In light of her convictions, the Supreme Court upheld a ruling which had denied Schwimmer's application for citizenship, stating that it was a fundamental duty to defend the government, by force of arms if need be. Holmes's dissent was strongly personalized. He declared the applicant to be "a woman of superior character and intelligence, obviously more than ordinarily desireable as a citizen." As for bearing arms, he saw her refusal as immaterial since "she is a woman over fifty years of age and would not be allowed to bear arms if she wanted to." Nor was Holmes concerned that in wartime she might espouse views designed to endanger the nation's security. "Her position and motives" he thought of "as wholly different from those of Schenck. She is an optimist and states in strong, and I do not doubt, sincere words her belief that war will disappear...." Only at the end of his opinion did Holmes introduce the argument that "the principle of free thought—not free thought for those who agree with us but freedom for the thought that we hate"—as an operative factor.[29] The *Schwimmer* dissent aroused a lot of sympathy, but as the justice replied to one admirer, "it was moral sympathy, not legal judgment" that led to praise of Holmes.[30] In fact it was Holmes who had made a moral judgment in the case. And in the privacy of his correspondence his intimation that Rosika Schwimmer's flamboyant declaration of atheism made the

Court's decision against her easier to pronounce also serves as a clue to his own attitude of support.[31]

IV   *Response to Normalcy*

The return to normalcy in the national outlook after World War I was not likely to be greeted by Holmes with equanimity. Many of his judicial determinants long and firmly established, like his penchant for social experimentation under the law, were to be challenged frequently over the last years of Holmes's justiceship. He and Brandeis found themselves together in dissent, though not always so, and in the process they questioned many of the assumptions and the tendencies in American life during the 1920s. In a sense, the lead in the partnership was to pass from Holmes to Brandeis as the decade wore on. In 1918 Holmes expressed himself as "catspawed by Brandeis to do another dissent on burning themes."[32] As he phrased it at a later time, "the ever-active Brandeis put upon my conscience the responsibility of another dissent."[33] Brandeis for his part deemed Holmes his indispensable support. With many of the issues coming before the Court Brandeis felt impelled to grapple. It was altogether impossible for him to affect indifference to the social conflicts which swirled and eddied about the Court. For Holmes it was easy not to get involved; because of age and temperament he often could not keep up with his "upward and outward" brother. He put it well in a letter to his friend in April 1919: "Generally speaking I agree with you in liking to see special experiments tried, but I do so without enthusiasm because I believe that it is merely shifting the place of pressure and that so long as we have free propagation Malthus is right in his general view."[34] At bottom it was their tolerance of social change which was the common ground of their agreement. But because the orientation of each judge was different—Holmes being philosophical-judicial and Brandeis being sociological-judicial— the two friends might well disagree in their judgments of a particular case.

Two cases illustrate their occasional differences, at the same time as such differences promote understanding of their respective judicial outlooks. One of these, *Bartels* v. *Iowa* (1922),[35] concerned a state law prohibiting the teaching of German to schoolchildren, one of the baleful results of patriotic excess common to World War I. Not surprisingly Brandeis voted with the majority of the Court, which declared such a law unconstitutional. But Holmes, "with hesitation and unwillingness," chose to differ. "No one would doubt," he argued, "that a teacher might be forbidden to teach many things," with the only constitutional criteria being whether "the statute passes the bounds of reason. . . ." As the facts of the case were those in which, in his judgment, men might reasonably differ, he was "unable to say that the Constitution of the United States prevents the experiment from being tried." By contrast, in *Pennsylvania Coal Company* v. *Mahon* (1922),[36] Holmes voted with the majority, which ruled that a state statute seeking to limit mining operations which threatened residential properties with cave-ins was bad law. "The general rule at least is that while property may be regulated to a certain extent, if regulation goes too far it will be recognized as taking." In this unusual invocation of a "general rule," it was, as usual, a "question of degree." Brandeis in dissent reminded the Court that the right of ownership was not absolute, that "uses, once harmless, may, owing to changed conditions, seriously threaten the public welfare." Even given such occasions for disagreement, Holmes and Brandeis ordinarily came down on the same side of a constitutional question.

With the passing years, the mood of the country and the Court became increasingly conservative. In *United States* v. *United States Steel Corporation* (1920),[37] the rule of reason was invoked, resulting in acceptance by the Court of that giant combination on the grounds of "economic legitimacy." Holmes, incidentally, concurred in the ruling written by Justice McKenna. But he was more likely to be true to his tolerance of social experimentation while resisting encroachments by the government on the rights of the individual. Several notable cases, *Truax* v. *Corrigan* (1921), *Adkins* v. *Children's Hospital* (1922), *Myers* v. *United States* (1926), and *Nixon* v. *Herndon* (1927), spoke aspects of Holmes the judge, but perhaps no more so than several lesser-known cases which provided him with added opportunity to put his mind to the socioeconomic problems generated by the decade of prosperity.

When the prerogatives of the nation and a state collided, as happened in *Wallace* v. *Himes* (1920),[38] Holmes declared that state actions interfering with interstate commerce were indefensible, the issue being a special excise tax levied on railroads doing business in North Dakota. "The purpose is not to expose the heel of the system [of interstate commerce] to a mortal dart," he complained. The tax was "an unwarranted interference with interstate commerce and a taking of property without due process"—all rather tame stuff by the 1920s. No less routine were his views in *Erie Railroad Company* v. *Public Utility Commission* (1921),[39] wherein he upheld the right of a state to insist that the public safety legitimately required a railroad corporation to maintain grade crossings in a manner not dangerous to the public, even at great and unanticipated expense to the corporation. Less predictably, Holmes in a dissenting opinion refused to allow that the Sherman Act's restrictions on combinations in restraint of trade should be applied to the American Hardwood Manufacturing Association (*American Column* v. *United States*, 1921).[40] He judged that the 365 members of the association merely exchanged information on sales, prices, and production. Information is not conspiracy, he asserted, "in a country of free speech that affects to regard education and knowledge as desirable." These and others demonstrate that Holmes continued mostly to offer judgment, as he understood the facts of the case.

V *Continuing to Dissent*

In two widely referred cases, *Truax* v. *Corrigan* and *Adkins* v. *Children's Hospital*, Holmes—and Brandeis as well—disputed the pronounced conservatism of the Court when deciding the rights of laborers under the Constitution. In *Truax* v. *Corrigan* (1921), a state law of Arizona, which prohibited injunctions in labor disputes, "intended and inflicted" a loss of property.[41] In the words of Chief Justice Taft, who spoke for the Court, "the Constitution was intended, its very purpose is, to prevent experimentation with fundamental rights of the individual property owner." Holmes deemed Taft's reasoning "spongy."[42] In dissent, he objected to treating business as property, contended that perhaps injunctions were more liable to abuse in labor disputes than elsewhere, and pointed out that, in any circumstance, the power of the state legislature should be respected. His summary statement had that typical sense of Olympian detachment:

I must add one general consideration. There is nothing I more deprecate than the use of the Fourteenth Amendment beyond the absolute compulsion of its words to prevent the making of social experiments that an important part of the community desires, in the insulated chambers afforded by the several states, even though the experiments may seem futile or even noxious to me and to those whose judgment I must respect.[43]

The next year, 1922, Holmes's judgment went athwart a majority refusal to sanction an act of Congress which established minimum wages for women working in the District of Columbia in *Adkins* v. *Children's Hospital*.[44] The issue raised was hardly an unfamiliar one,—liberty of contract. Justice Sutherland's majority opinion appealed to the *Adair*, the *Coppage*, and the *Lochner* decisions, while the dissenters (who included both Taft and Holmes, though in separate opinions) quoted approvingly from *Bunting* v. *Oregon* and *Muller* v. *Oregon*. Holmes's analysis of the facts and the law was a point by point refutation of the position taken by the Court. To him the power of the Congress was "absolutely free from doubt," and the means utilized long approved. As for violation of the due process clause of the Fifth Amendment, it became a matter of judgment which had to be made in light of long-established laws against usury, against fraud, against Sunday sales, even—all of which in some way interfered with liberty of contract. He scored the inconsistency of the Court in its acceptance of maximum hours (*Muller* v. *Oregon*) and its rejection of minimum wages, along with the majority's argument that the Nineteenth Amendment in effect had deprived women of any special privilege before the law in cases of liberty of contract. Holmes directly attacked the arguments from the Nineteenth Amendment, contending that the right of women to vote had not erased differences between the sexes in the labor market. Furthermore, he pointed out that the law in question did not "compel anybody to pay anything. It simply forbids employment at rates below those fixed as the minimum requirement of healthy and right living." Finally, Holmes made his appeal that "reasonable men" might well agree that such a law was useful.[45] All in all, he offered no new interpretations beyond his comments on the limits of the Nineteenth Amendment. But he did pass judgment in a particular case based on interpretations long established.

Holmes's respect for the will of the legislature received fresh expression in a case dealing with the authority of the Congress, *Myers* v. *United States* (1926).[46] According to an 1876 statute, Congress granted the president the power to name first-class postmasters as part of a law establishing grades of post offices within the postal service. The president's authority to appoint and to remove was contingent on the advice and consent of the Senate. In 1920 President Wilson removed the postmaster of Portland, Oregon, without consulting the Senate. While a majority of the Court, including a former chief executive, Taft, had no difficulty approving this action, neither Holmes nor Brandeis agreed. The executive power as such, and arguments drawn from it, were "Spiders' webs inadequate to control the dominant facts," in Holmes's phrase. Postmasterships depended on Congress alone. Congress conferred the power to appoint and thus rightfully might require approval of the Senate to remove. It was the duty of the president to execute the law. The executive power and the legislative power in some sense were intertwined, in other words. Holmes contended for much the same principle in *Springer* v. *Philippine Islands* (1927)[47] when he said, "the great ordinances of the Constitution do not establish and divide fields of black and white." The right of the Filipino legislature to create boards of control for banks and other enterprises, like the authority of the Congress to supervise the removal of postmasters, "fall into the indiscriminate residue of matters within legislative control."[48]

In the 1920s, when the rights of black citizens were abrogated or neglected, Holmes took a liberal position. One such example was the case *Moore* v. *Dempsey* (1923).[49] Mob action, which had made impossible a fair trial for five blacks accused of killing a white man in Arkansas, was judged to violate the due-process clause of the Fourteenth Amendment. The facts in the legal processes appeared incontrovertible. Tensions ran high in the community where the trial was held, blacks had been systematically excluded from the jury, counsel for the defense made no plea for delay or change of venue, witnesses for the defense were not called, the trial lasted three-quarters of an hour, and the jury deliberated five minutes before bringing in a verdict of guilty of murder in the first degree. The Supreme Court concluded that such a series of procedures failed to meet the requirements of a due process and a new trial was ordered. In a second case, *Nixon v. Herndon* (1927),[50] the court ruled against a Texas law denying to blacks eligibility in a Democratic primary as contrary to the selfsame Fourteenth Amendment. Quoting *Strauder v. West Virginia,* Holmes, for a unanimous Court, wrote that the "statute of Texas in the teeth of prohibitions . . . assumes to forbid Negroes to take part in a primary election, the importance of which we have indicated, discrimination . . . by distinction of color alone. . . ." "It is clear . . . that color can not be made the basis of a statutory classification affecting the right [to vote]."

While it may be useful to note that Holmes in his words was hewing closely to the law literally construed in these two cases, a deep sense of concern over such constitutional violations pervaded his total view. The liberal accents with which he spoke were unmistakable. Prepared to extend the authority of due process in the area of citizen rights, he was unwilling to allow the Fourteenth Amendment to restrict what he thought of as the legitimate sphere of state legislature in matters like taxation. His reason for so judging was given fresh statement in 1930 in *Baldwin v. Missouri*: "As the decisions now stand I see hardly any limit but the sky to the invalidating of those rights if they happen to strike a majority of the Court as for any reason undesirable. I cannot believe that the Amendment was intended to give us *carte blanche* to embody our economic or moral beliefs in its prohibitions."[51] Such words were not an illiberal rendering of a philosophical-judicial opinion, and an appropriate departing thought on Oliver Wendell Holmes, judge.

CHAPTER 7

Neither Liberal nor Conservative

I Liberal/Conservative Axis

THE question remains: was Oliver Wendell Holmes liberal or conservative? In retirement he persisted in his lifelong search for a better understanding of man against the cosmos, a reconsideration of final things. One of his last published letters, to Pollock, spoke of the "possibility of writing a little book embodying my views on the ultimates of the law." Had he done so, it would have been generously sprinkled with *aperçus*. A concluding statement on Holmes therefore needs to be rendered in philosophical no less than in legal terms. Any exploration of the question, liberal or conservative, must proceed over legal and philosophical ground. In particular, Holmes's preoccupation with the nature of truth invites examination along a liberal/conservative axis.

Both liberals and conservatives can lay claim to Holmes as a worthy exemplar and influential spokesman of a point of view. His defense of freedom of speech can be nicely balanced by warnings he offered against "tinkering with the institution of private property." Dissent in the *Abrams* case has an appropriate analogue in *Bailey* v. *Alabama* (1911), for example, with its forthright statement in support of the sacredness of a contract once entered into. Curiously, however, Holmes has won his disciples from among the liberals, despite an impressive amount of evidence giving credence to a conservative Mr. Justice Holmes. Conservatives have chosen to attack his liberalism rather than to celebrate those elements in his thought which are susceptible to a congenial interpretation.[1] The debate concerning his public philosophy also has been explored at a more subtle level: the positivism of his legal mind as distinguished from a sympathy

135

for a higher law, the starting point of legal conservatives. Such considerations have occasioned a repudiation of liberal and conservative labels as irrelevant—if not unworthy of the subject and the man—though the categories remain.[2] As for the justice himself, this interlacing of seemingly opposed legal attitudes should not suggest that he desired to appear all things to all men. Holmes was not often consciously liberal or conservative in his judicial role. To his own satisfaction he was able, nevertheless, to maintain basic distinctions which have yielded to either liberal or conservative constructions. Had he failed to do so, the resulting admixture surely would have made him little different from many of the other associates of his day, who discharged their duties responsibly enough without making much of an impact along the way. It may be allowed to remain unsettled, for the moment at least, whether by persisting in this duality Holmes united in his outlook the diverging intellectual streams of evolutionary determinism and problem-solving pragmatism, or merely exhibited his own reluctance to come down on one side or the other of what was a perennial problem for him—the nature of truth. More immediately important, Holmes's final inability to reach a personal commitment to the proper mode of achieving truth, and the ongoing struggle during his shaping years and after to resolve this dilemma, energized both liberal and conservative instincts when it came to the law. The action was reciprocal: the intellectual appeal of one mode of reaching truth served to remind him of the demands of the other.[3]

The liberal/conservative dichotomy discernible in the corpus of his Supreme Court rulings arose directly from what was at heart a philosophical issue. Holmes developed an attitude toward truth-finding which included both historical-analytical and scientific-methodological means of verification. Truth in law, in other words, could be determined by its evolution, which comprised tangibles and intangibles. But truth also must be tested by its pertinence, its timeliness, its applicability. There were certainly pressure points between these diverse lines of inquiry. By incorporating features from each, Holmes succumbed to the blandishments of neither. The basis of tension between the two views of understanding lay in the difficulty imposed by the human lack of certitude and the disputability of the power of verification. A determinability growing out of an evolutionary order, as Holmes early perceived it, competed with the salient advantages of an open-ended universe implicit in his pragmatism. The question which was to be one of the most relevant for Holmes in the whole range of his intellectual concerns was how to make a theory of living, and thus a theory of law, viable without deforming stability and order. From his varying response to the question, disciples and opponents have fashioned liberal and conservative estimates.

II *Philosophical Roots*

The distinction Holmes drew between the cosmological and the phenomenal, which was central to his thinking, also discloses the liberal/conservative pattern. The cosmological he associated with principles and final truths, knowledge which he questioned as beyond the scope and power of human reason. The connotations of the cosmological were related to the ordinances and prescriptions of theology and philsophy to *a priori*'s and absolute necessity—all of which repelled Holmes. The phenomenal, in contrast, was that order of the universe called natural, and as such was discernible by scientific methods. The scientific universe included within it evolutionary as well as pragmatic strains of thought. In such a context the influence of positivism, with its insistence on the exclusion of all but the scientifically determinable properties of the universe as suitable for study, had great meaning for Holmes. He was to remain deeply in its debt, especially in terms of the reverence with which he held the scientific method as a means of problem-solving. He took the position that the scientist, "given time and painstaking research, could be reasonably expected to solve all problems."[4]

Holmes consistently redirected attention to a comparative evaluation of the scientific method of discovery, with its dependence on quantitative determination, and the historical method, with its understanding of the subtleties of tradition, custom, and ethos. In his early years, he recognized the prospect of irreconcilability between the two methods, which he chose to put in terms of the growth and functioning of the law rather than according to the nature of man's thought. But as law is a reflection of things human, it can do no more, and no less, than embody its sources. In *The Common Law* Holmes remarked that "the truth in the law is always approaching and never reaching consistency. . . . It will become entirely consistent only when it ceases to grow." Holmes delighted in constantly molding and adapting, as thought and experience accumulated. Though he believed fundamentally in the efficacy of thought and the necessity of reason over disorder, he also appreciated the requirements imposed by custom and public opinion, and the limitations on freedom of thought derived from history and tradition.

III *Variant Inclinations*

Oliver Wendell Holmes's personal philosophy often disclosed variant inclinations toward the scientific and historical formulas. Incompatibility stalked him when critical issues surfaced. The evolutionary thesis not only plagued moral notions from the past but called into question the theory of pragmatic problem-solving. He found himself in a complex dilemma over the nature of truth: was it cosmological or phenomenal? This, in turn, affected his method of determining truth: was it by scientific experimentation or historical investigation? Whereupon Holmes had to resolve a final question: who or what was the agent of determination: the individual or society? If the truth in law was phenomenal, it was susceptible to scientific investigation and determination by a citizen or a group of citizens. But if the individual or social element in the law added a degree of the cosmological, then the law indeed became a maze of reason and unreason, of history and new ideas. As Holmes grew older, he was increasingly attracted to the second possibility, and at times became overwhelmed by the inscrutable nature of truth. But he maintained a steadfastness in making decisions in spite of uncertainty over the method, if only because of what he discovered in the realities of life. Largely as a matter of practicality, Holmes accepted the law as both cosmological and phenomenal. Its cosmological aspect was due at root to human agents as participants and to "competing social ends," values which depended on the imponderables of history and sentiment. On the other side, the law could and should strive for increasing precision. To a greater or lesser extent, Holmes thought, some quantitative analysis could be made, though the analysis would not thereby preclude the necessity of exercising final human judgments.

Holmes had to accept what he noted early in *The Common Law*, that the law was a mixture of history and new ideas. Neither historical perspectives nor scientific investigations alone guaranteed a wisdom of judgment in as much as there could be honest, indeed, profound disagreement over which of the two methods might be the more appropriate to apply in given cir-- cumstances. Hopefully, reason and common sense could be useful tools in bringing understanding to evaluation. The process should assume that "historical continuity is only a necessity, not a duty," as Holmes was fond of quoting, and recognize that the law must be open-ended, taking advantage of fresh concepts, new experience, and imaginative insights. In short, for Holmes, there must be a dynamic tension between precedent and the imperative of social experiment, between a conservative and a liberal psychology. He continued to believe that his own thoughts were well founded, of course, but he admitted that there was no sound reason for assuming them to be eternal truths, "that the ultimates of a little creature on this little earth are the last word of the unimaginable whole." Bred in a tradition which placed so much emphasis on individual salvation gained through personal awareness, his response to a future described by science revealed an ambiguity which he perforce carried over into his legal achievement.

The inability of Oliver Wendell Holmes to come to a belief in any discernible absolutes, or to be capable of precise evaluation of all events in the phenomenal world, imposed an added weight to the third and final question relating to the nature of truth. Does truth reside more effectively in the individual or in the community? Such a dichotomy bears directly on conservative as opposed to liberal preferences. To this problem Holmes brought different temperaments, which depended on how much he was willing to accede to one point of view or the other. One manner in which he looked at truth—as a force conquering all opposing force—was one of objective appreciation. While he remained aware and insistent in behalf of his own subjective beliefs, at the same time he attempted to give them some measure of further validity with his "can't help" proposition. When Holmes fell back on his "can't helps," he did so ordinarily to support his belief in the phenomenal as distinct from the cosmological. It is a misreading of the total Holmes, however, to confine his "can't helps" to the phenomenal, thus excluding them from the moral order. When he opposed child labor, he did so because he could not help believe that child labor was an abuse; when he upheld free speech, he did so because he could not help think that its denial was vicious; when he proclaimed against government wire-tapping to obtain evidence, he was heard because he could not help judge the action ignoble. The "can't helps" functioned readily as a conscience, though they also were useful to challenge unscientific postulates about man and the cosmos. The "can't helps" enabled Holmes to appear liberal or conservative. But because his "can't helps" were invoked as they were he was, in effect, neither liberal nor conservative, but Holmesian.

The tension arising regarding truth measured on a social rather than a subjective scale imposed on this third level of truth an awareness of the problem of the uses of majoritarian rule. The clash between collectivist and individualist notions of truth produced psychological fluctuations in Holmes. He lacked a clearly conceived and consistently stated commitment to which type of truth he thought best founded. In his personal philosophy he preferred individual judgment; in his legal philosophy he came to adopt a collectivist stand and to accept that, for society as a whole, the force of the public will should be paramount. "The truth seems to me," he stated in *Tyson* v. *Banton* (1927), "that subject to compensation when compensation is due, the legislature may forbid or restrict any business when it has sufficient force of public opinion behind it."[5] The reference to compensation comes as a reminder that for Holmes individual rights died hard. On any one decision, to be sure, he invoked force, majority rule, or felt necessities as determinants of truth. For society at large (which Holmes did not believe required those rock-ribbed and immutable verities for which the individual was known to crave), the wiser course was to follow a viable, experimental way to truth. Truth in law was largely prescribed, or ought to be, by public opinion, yet Holmes frequently verified public opinion by his subjective "can't helps."

Perhaps the central difficulty in assessing Holmes's understanding of truth is that he did not give much evidence of having evaluated in a firm manner the relative worth of the individual creed and the collective program. He made assessments of the two, but he tended to put them in terms of a present which could change drastically. An interesting example of his equivocation on public questions was his oft-quoted remark to John W. Davis, solicitor general of the United States, after the latter had offered argument in an antitrust case. "Of course, I know and every other sensible man knows that the Sherman Law is damned nonsense, but if my country wants to go to hell, I am here to help it." Holmes's strong leaning toward the social Darwinist view of life as an individual struggle for assertion (and hence his belief that truth was demonstrable in certain circumstances and always in behalf of a superior force) was apparent when he said,

I believe that Malthus was right in his fundamental notion and that is as far as we have got or are likely to get in my day. Every society is founded on the death of men. . . . I shall think that socialism begins to be entitled to serious treatment when and not before it takes life in hand and prevents the continuance of the unfit.[6]

Still, Holmes hesitated in his judicial function to impose his own inclinations too thoroughly on the law. In fact, he warned persistently against the violation of the standard he considered most necessary—that juridical neutrality was dependent on juridical impartiality:

It is a misfortune if a judge reads his conscious or unconscious sympathy with one side or the other into the law, and forgets that what seems to him to be first principles are believed by half of his fellow men to be wrong.[7]

More importantly, Holmes went on to challenge in bold fashion whether the nature of the impenetrable cosmos, about which he often spoke, did not preclude men from certitude even about their firmest convictions:

I think that we have suffered from this misfortune in state courts, at least, and that this is another and very important truth to be extracted from popular discontent. When twenty years ago a vague terror went over the earth and the word socialism began to be heard, I thought and still think that fear was translated into doctrines that had no place in the Constitution or the common law. Judges are apt to be naif, simple-minded men, and they need something of Mephistopheles. We too need education in the obvious—to learn to transcend our own convictions and to leave room for much that we hold dear to be done away with short of revolution by the orderly change of law.[8]

Such a passage from Holmes demonstrates how both history and science attracted him in nearly equal measure.

Holmes was an evolutionist who refused to accept the finality or unconditionality of any proposition. His hesitancy to adopt final standards was a logical outcome of his skepticism. It reflected even more the essential humility which his investigations of cosmic truth had demanded of him. Though an individual could and often did hold to many fixed beliefs (and Holmes himself did not differ in this respect), men ought not to embody these beliefs with the same degree of personal assurance when discussing legal questions whose effects reached beyond the individual who was pronouncing them. For Holmes, certitude "was not the test of certainty."[9] Since in many ways the appointment of judges was an accident of history, it was in some sense undesirable to have the "first principles" of "naif, simple-minded men" formalized into law. Even these judges whose brilliance and farsightedness were beyond question had no claim to expect that their decisions would be necessarily of permanent applicability, given the vagaries of history and the shifting ground on which such judgments were based. For practical reasons, "the first requirement of a sound body of law is that it should correspond with the actual feelings and demands of the community whether right or wrong." As there was no ultimate guarantee of certitude, the development of society should be properly left in its legal ramifications to the collective will as demonstrated in the "sufficient force of public opinion."

IV *Derivative Principles*

In terms of a theory of law, Holmes placed greatest emphasis on three derivative principles. First, that judicial impartiality was necessitated by the human inability to achieve cosmic truth. As Felix Frankfurter has observed in his discussion of Holmes, "the nature of the Court's tasks raises the crucial problem of our constitutional system in that its successful operation calls for rare intellectual disinterestedness and penetration, lest limitation in personal experience and imagination operate as limitations on the Constitution."[10] Second, the Court had only the duty to judge whether a man has cause to believe the reasonableness of his arguments, not whether the judges themselves believe his argument to be wise. Historical conditions require the introduction of new techniques and the determination of the advisability of each innovation, not as a function of immutable principles of inherent rightness, but of trial. Third, that new understanding of law was best accomplished when respecting those past traditions which possessed continued value. In concrete cases, Holmes contended that the term "liberty," for example, had to be given great latitude of meaning, bounded only by clear violations that would "infringe principles as they have been understood by the traditions of our people and our law." Without looking upon custom as anything more than an obligatory part of any opinion, Holmes attempted to foster a newer and more organic concept of law. His introduction of scientific ways into the decision-making processes of the courts elicited another example of how he thought the law ought to, and indeed must, take advantage of experience without abandoning all past understandings. Most of all, he thought that an evolutionist who emphasized the nature of truth, at the same stroke, would welcome an increasing rationalization of the law, giving it directed purpose and greater accuracy of expression.

V *Power of Constructive Negation*

In spite of the fact that Mr. Justice Holmes voted with the majority at a ratio of eight or ten to one, he derived much of his historical importance from the dissents he voiced. Holmes was one of the few men who molded public opinion by the power of constructive negation. Remarkably, he was less successful in persuading others to adopt the same line of legal thought as he himself espoused. There were disciples like Justice Frankfurter, not to mention kindred judges like Louis D. Brandeis. More often, however, Holmes's stirring phrases and derisive opinions captured the fancy and the conviction of the listener only on the point he was making. Chief Justice Taft's dissent in the *Adkins* v. *Children's Hospital* reflected this, for example: unable to assign his signature to the dissenting opinion of Holmes because he could not bring himself to agree with some of the basic principles expressed therein, Taft nonetheless agreed that the case should not have been decided on the logic of the *Lochner* case of 1905 and the sanctity of property over human concerns. Arguing that the *Lochner* decision on which the majority had based its views had been overturned, Taft went on to note that the *Adkins* decision expressed an economic rather than a judicial perspective: "It is not the function of this court to hold congressional acts invalid simply because they are passed to carry out the economic views which the Court believed to be unwise and unsound."[11] Not only had Taft come to the same conclusion as had Holmes in this case, but he resorted to words which closely resembled those of Holmes in his *Lochner* opinion, wherein the latter had remarked that "the constitution is not intended to embody a particular economic theory, whether of paternalism . . . or of laissez-faire."

Oliver Wendell Holmes's greatest influence grew out of a feeling or temperament which rejected the traditional school of judicial obstructionism. His basic philosophical disposition was not clearly mirrored in those who agreed with his conclusions. In large part, this can be attributed to Holmes's personal inability to resolve the thorny issue of subjective truth, the shape of the universe, and the potency of man to determine it. His philosophical beliefs, moreover, were of such a sort as to produce a sardonic rather than a magnetic personality, and this in turn militated against any inclination Holmes might have harbored to be an active reformer. He understood himself perfectly in this matter: "Four years on the Bench was worth a lifetime in the Presidency," he remarked to one close friend.[12] And Francis Biddle has written of him: "He was an aristocrat and a conservative. He did not prefer, he said, a world with a hundred million bores in it to one with ten."[13] If Holmes never offered a social policy of his own and was without a definite credo to spark a nation's imagination, he never could hope to be more than an intellectual legalist and seer: "The thing I have wanted to do and wanted to do is to put as many new ideas into the law as I can, to show how particular solutions involve general theory."[14] It was this very desire to put new ideas into the law, and the attending success of that endeavor, which has made Holmes controversial. But there should be no controversy about his liberal versus his conservative outlook. In the accepted sense of being committed to one or the other, irrespective of the changing meanings of such labels, he preferred not to bother. His unsettled notions on truth and how to achieve it underscore the chief source of his restraint and detachment as a jurist; they may also explain in some measure why he was unable to enunciate a social policy. So much of what critics have found to praise and to condemn in Justice Holmes is bound up on his dual response to the nature and the methods of truth.

VI *Authorship Summarized*

Oliver Wendell Holmes, Jr., was most prominently jurist, philosopher, and historian. Essential to each of these roles was Holmes the author. Writing was not an unconscious occupation. In the law reports he was aware that what he said and how he said it could have long-standing consequences. Holmes was not inclined to take a back seat to many of his contemporaries in estimating his own importance. His judicial opinions, therefore, were nearly always crafted with a view to enhancing their impact, and when he had to deal with abstruse legal matters he made real efforts to translate technicalities into comprehensible language. The sum of his judicial opinions adds up to several volumes, and therein can be found short essays as part of his judgments on a wide variety of social, economic, and political issues. Holmes's work as a writer is perhaps more directly apparent in the learned essays he produced for various occasions. Among these, "The Path of the Law" (1897), "Law in Science and Science in Law" (1899), and "Natural Law" (1918) are significant contributions to jurisprudential literature. In these and other essays Holmes was not nearly so eager to democratize his

language. He was writing for the legal mind and in that capacity
kept his style on a high plain. He was rarely verbose. His instinct
for the trenchant phrase common to his judicial opinions finds
its counterpart in the lean and disciplined prose of his learned
essays. Finally, *The Common Law*, which must figure prominently in any account of Holmes the legal authority, also con-
firms him as an important American author. Justice Holmes was
one of the few men who could make literature out of the law.
As it was, he left unwritten a short book of reflections on the
law.[15] Such a project, though never carried out, does suggest
that Holmes thought himself a man of letters.

VII *"The Job of Life"*

Oliver Wendell Holmes, Jr., died in March 1935, two days
before his ninety-fourth birthday. His life had been a long and a
prosperous one in the ways he counted most valuable. He was
lonely after the death of his wife in 1929, and lonelier still when
he retired from the Court, for Fanny Holmes and the justiceship
had been his great personal prizes. An old man may be allowed
reflections on death, especially his own. In one of the memorable
passages of his letters to Pollock, Holmes wrote:

But as life draws to an end (one never quite believes it), I think
rather more than ever that man has respected himself too much and
the universe too little. He has thought himself a god and has despised
"brute matter," instead of thinking his importance to be all of one
piece with the rest. But the carnal man still is strong within me
and I take a good deal of interest in the job—the job of life.[16]

"The job of life," Holmes's fascination with it, endured to the
very end.

Notes and References

Some readers may be unfamiliar with the citations of law-report material which appear at various points in these notes. All of these citations follow the same format: the first number cited is a reference to the volume; "Mass." or "U.S." refers to the appropriate set of reports in which the volume appears; the next number refers to the page in the volume; and the number in parentheses is the year in which the case was heard.

Chapter One

1. Learned Hand, "Mr. Justice Holmes," *Mr. Justice Holmes*, Felix Frankfurter, ed. (New York, 1931), p. 131.

2. Oliver Wendell Holmes, "The Puritans," *Speeches* (Boston, 1913), p. 21.

3. The phrase of Samuel Eliot Morison in *The Maritime History of Massachusetts* (Boston and New York, 1921), p. 188.

4. Holmes to Patrick Augustine Sheehan, Oct. 27, 1912, *Holmes-Sheehan Correspondence*, David H. Burton, ed. (Port Washington, N.Y., 1976), p. 51.

5. Holmes to Sir Frederick E. Pollock, June 20, 1928, *Holmes-Pollock Letters*, Mark deW. Howe, ed., 2 vols. (Cambridge, Mass., 1941), II, 223.

6. Van Wyck Brooks, *New England: Indian Summer 1865–1915* (New York, 1940), looks back from 1865 to "Dr. Holmes's Boston." See pp. 1–22.

7. The phrase is that of Charles S. Peirce as applied to absolutes in philosophy. *Collected Papers of Charles S. Peirce*, Charles Hartshorne and Paul Weiss, eds., 6 vols. (Cambridge, Mass., 1933–1935), I, 357. Peirce was a close friend of Holmes during the days of the Metaphysical Club, 1868ff.

8. Quoted in Frederick C. Fiechter, Jr., "The Preparation of an American Aristocrat," *The New England Quarterly* VI: 1 (March, 1933): 3–28.

9. Ibid., p. 4.

10. There are useful genealogical tables dealing with Holmes's

descent and his mother's family in Catherine Drinker Bowen, *Yankee From Olympus* (Boston, 1944), pp. 6, 80. See also Silas Bent, *Justice Oliver Wendell Holmes* (New York, 1932), p. 26, and Mark deW. Howe, *Justice Oliver Wendell Holmes, Jr., The Shaping Years, 1841–1870* (Cambridge, Mass., 1957), pp. 31–32.

11. Bowen, p. 100.

12. Arnold L. Goldsmith, "Oliver Wendell Holmes Father and Son," *Journal of Criminal Law, Criminology and Political Science* 48:4 (Nov.-Dec. 1957): 394–98 passim.

13. Bowen, p. 81.

14. Quoted in Howe, p. 5.

15. Fiechter, pp. 7–8.

16. Holmes to Sheehan, Aug. 14, 1911, *Holmes-Sheehan Correspondence*, p. 44.

17. Bent, p. 45.

18. Holmes, "The Class of '61," *Speeches*, p. 96.

19. Holmes to Pollock, Dec. 7, 1927, *Holmes-Pollock Letters*, II, 207.

20. Bent, pp. 42–43.

21. Ibid., p. 69.

22. Holmes, "Harvard College at War," *Speeches*, p. 14.

23. Howe's chapter, "Harvard College," is best relied on for an awareness of this aspect of Holmes's background; see Howe, *The Shaping Years*, pp. 35–79.

24. Holmes, *Touched with Fire*, Mark deW. Howe, ed. (Cambridge, Mass., 1947), p. 32.

25. Howe, *The Shaping Years*, p. 62.

26. Ibid., p. 44.

27. Ibid., p. 45.

28. Holmes to Sheehan, July 17, 1909, *Holmes-Sheehan Correspondence*, pp. 27–28.

29. Holmes, "Plato," *University Quarterly* II: 1 (Oct. 1860): 205–17 passim.

30. Quoted in Howe, *The Shaping Years*, p. 54.

31. Holmes, "Plato," p. 210.

32. Holmes, "Notes on Albert Dürer," reprinted in Wolfgang Stechow, "Justice Holmes' Notes on Albert Dürer," *Journal of Aesthetics and Art Criticism* VII: 2 (Dec. 1949): 119–24.

33. Ibid., p. 119.

34. Holmes to Amelia Jackson Holmes, Oct. 23, 1861, *Touched with Fire*, p. 13. This volume includes the wartime letters of Holmes as well as portions of his diary for 1861–1864, and as such is the

major source for understanding the effects of the Civil War on Holmes.

35. Holmes to Harold J. Laski, May 4, 1924, *Holmes-Laski Letters,* Mark deW. Howe, ed. 2 vols. (Cambridge, Mass., 1953), I, 615.

36. Holmes to parents, Sept. 18, 1862, *Touched with Fire,* p. 64.

37. Holmes to Pollock, Dec. 21, 1886, *Holmes-Pollock Letters,* I, 29.

38. Holmes to Laski, Dec. 16, 1926, *Holmes-Laski Letters,* II, 905.

39. George M. Frederickson, *The Inner Civil War* (New York, 1968), p. 172.

40. Holmes to his mother, Oct. 23, 1861, *Touched with Fire,* p. 13.

41. Holmes to his father, Dec. 20, 1862, *Touched with Fire,* p. 80.

42. Holmes, "Memorial Day," *Speeches,* p. 8.

43. Holmes to his mother, June 7, 1864, *Touched with Fire,* p. 143 (italics in original).

44. Holmes to Charles Eliot Norton, April 17, 1864, quoted in *Touched with Fire,* p. 122, n. 1.

45. Holmes, "The Soldiers' Faith," *Speeches,* p. 58.

46. Holmes to Lewis Einstein, *The Holmes-Einstein Letters,* James B. Peabody, ed. (New York, 1964), p. xvi.

47. Howe, *The Shaping Years,* p. 86.

48. See especially Touster, *In Search of Holmes from Within,* VAND. LAW REV., 438 (1964–1965).

49. Holmes to Lewis Einstein, April 12, 1925, *The Holmes-Einstein Letters,* p. 235.

50. Holmes to his mother, Dec. 15, 1862, *Touched with Fire,* p. 78.

51. Holmes to his parents, May 16, 1864, *Touched with Fire,* pp. 122–23.

52. Holmes Diary, *Touched with Fire,* pp. 27–28.

53. Holmes to his father, March 29, 1863, *Touched with Fire,* pp. 90–91.

Chapter Two

1. Bowen, pp. 198ff; Howe, *The Proving Years* (Cambridge, Mass., 1963), pp. 176ff. Inasmuch as both Bowen and Howe offer evidence for their contrasting views I have attempted to reconcile their differences.

2. Holmes, "Autobiographical Sketch," in *The Mind and Faith of Justice Holmes,* Max Lerner, ed. (Boston, 1943), p. 8.

3. Bowen, p. 198.

4. Ibid., p. 442; the quotation is ascribed to Laski.

5. Ibid., p. 253.

6. Bent, p. 127.

7. Howe, *The Shaping Years*, pp. 176, 304, n. 4.

8. Holmes, "The Uses of Law Schools," *Collected Legal Papers* (New York, 1920), p. 39.

9. Holmes, Review of "Introduction to the General Survey . . . ," *Collected Legal Papers*, p. 300.

10. Bowen, p. 203.

11. Southern Pacific Railway Company v. Jensen, 244 U.S. 205, 222 (1917).

12. Interesting material relative to the self-image is to be found in Maxwell Bloomfield, "Law v. Politics: The Self-Image of the American Bar (1830–1860)," in *Essays in Nineteenth Century Legal History*, Wythe Holt, ed. (Westport, Conn., 1976), pp. 706–23; Gerard W. Gawalt, "Massachusetts Legal Education in Transition, 1766–1840," ibid., pp. 650–73.

13. Bowen, p. 227.

14. New York Trust v. Eisner, 256 U.S. 345 (1920).

15. Howe, *The Shaping Years*, p. 250.

16. Ralph Barton Perry, *The Thought and Character of William James*, 2 vols. (Boston, 1935), I, 510.

17. Howe, *The Shaping Years*, p. 257.

18. Bowen, pp. 221–22.

19. Holmes, Review of "The Law Magazine and Review," 6 AM. L. REV. 723, 724 (1872).

20. Holmes, "The Path of the Law, *Collected Legal Papers*, p. 173.

21. For a fuller account of this contention see Max H. Fisch, "Justice Holmes, The Predictive Theory of Law and Pragmatism," *Journal of Philosophy* XXXIX: 4 (Feb. 12, 1942): 85–97. Holmes and pragmatism are usefully placed in a larger setting in Philip P. Wiener, *Evolution and the Founders of Pragmatism* (New York, 1949), pp. 173ff.

22. Perry, I, 519.

23. Howe, *The Shaping Years*, p. 315, n. 99.

24. Holmes, "Codes and the Arrangement of the Law," *Justice Oliver Wendell Holmes, His Book Notices and Uncollected Letters and Papers*, Harry C. Shriver, ed. (New York, 1936), pp. 66–67.

25. Holmes, Review of "Science of Legal Judgments," ibid., pp. 6–7.

26. Holmes, Review of "English Mind on Roman Law," ibid., pp. 16–17.

27. Holmes, Review of *Roscoe's Digests of the Law of Evidence in Criminal Cases*, 1 Am. L. Rev., 375.

28. Quoted in Howe, *The Shaping Years*, p. 268.

29. Holmes, *Summary of Events*, 2 Am. L. Rev. 547, 560 (1968).

30. Holmes to Laski, Sept. 15, 1916, *Holmes-Laski Letters*, I, 21.

31. Holmes, *The Gas Stokers' Strike*, 7 Am. L. Rev. 582, 583 (1873).

Chapter Three

1. Bowen, p. 270.

2. Howe, *The Proving Years*, p. 135.

3. Ibid., p. 101.

4. *Holmes-Pollock Letters*, 2nd edition, I, xxxix–xxx.

5. Ibid., pp. 3–4.

6. See Paul F. Boller, Jr., *American Thought in Transition* (Chicago, 1969), pp. 152–57.

7. Morton J. Horwitz, "The Emergence of an Instrumental Conception of American Law," *Essays in Nineteenth Century Legal History* (Cambridge, Mass., 1977) p. 105.

8. Howe, *The Proving Years*, p. 146.

9. Ibid., p. 136, n. 2.

10. Holmes, *The Common Law*, p. 5. All further references to this work in this chapter are provided in parentheses in the text and are taken from *The Common Law*, Mark DeW. Howe, ed. (Boston, 1963).

11. See Allen, *Criminal Law*, 31 U. Chi. L. Rev. 257 (1964), for a latter-day assessment of Holmes's treatment of criminal law in *The Common Law*.

12. Kalven discusses Holmes on Torts in *Torts*, 31 U. Chi. L. Rev. 263 (1964).

13. Sharp, *Contracts*, 31 U. Chi. L. Rev. 268 (1964), analyzes Holmes's treatment of contracts in *The Common Law*.

14. Frederic W. Maitland, *Collected Papers of Frederic W. Maitland* (London, 1911), II, 8.

15. The Harvard professional period is fully discussed in Howe, *The Proving Years*, pp. 252–82.

16. Howe, p. 281.

17. Holmes to James Bryce, Aug. 17, 1879, quoted in Howe, p. 280.

18. Howe, *The Proving Years*, p. 253.

Chapter Four

1. "I expect to be rather an anchorite this winter, and neither drink wine nor make love but to be happy and content if I am able to do my work and keep well." Holmes to Lady Pollock, Oct. 21, 1891, *Holmes-Pollock Letters,* I, 41.

2. Holmes to Pollock, March 9, 1884, *Holmes-Pollock Letters,* I, 25; Holmes to Pollock, Jan. 17, 1887, *Holmes-Pollock Letters,* I, 30.

3. Holmes, "The Path of the Law," *Collected Legal Papers,* p. 171.

4. Ibid., p. 194.

5. Holmes, "The Soldiers' Faith," *The Holmes Reader,* Julius Marke, ed. (Dobbs Ferry, N. Y., 1963), p. 102.

6. Ibid., p. 105.

7. Ibid., p. 102.

8. Ibid., p. 103. The lines quoted are from "Sir Launcelot and Queen Guinevere."

9. Holmes, "Law in Science and Science in Law," *Collected Legal Papers,* p. 242.

10. Holmes, "The Path of the Law," *Collected Legal Papers,* p. 200.

11. Holmes, "The Law," *The Holmes Reader,* p. 62.

12. Ibid.

13. 170 Mass. 596 (1897–1898).

14. 150 Mass. 194 (1889–1890).

15. 177 Mass. 485 (1900–1901).

16. Commonwealth v. Sullivan, 164 Mass. 144 (1895).

17. Fay v. Harrington, 176 Mass. 275 (1900); see also Holmes to Pollock, Oct. 21, 1895, *Holmes-Pollock Letters,* I, 65.

18. Holmes to Lady Pollock, Sept. 6, 1902, ibid., I, 105.

19. Hemenway v. Hemenway, 134 Mass. 449–450 (1883).

20. Heard v. Sturges, 146 Mass. 548 (1888).

21. Commonwealth v. Kennedy, 170 Mass. 20 (1897–1898).

22. Commonwealth v. Pierce, 138 Mass. 175–176, 179 (1884–1885); see also Holmes's dissent in Hadley P. Hanson v. Globe Newspaper Company, 159 Mass. 293 (1893), for a further example of the external standard concept.

23. 173 Mass. 286 (1899).

24. 149 Mass. 287, 289 (1889).

25. Smith v. Dickinson, 140 Mass. 172–173 (1885–1886).

26. Brigham v. Fayerweather, 140 Mass. 413 (1885–1886).

27. Rideout v. Knox, 148 Mass. 372–373 (1888–1889).

28. Ibid., 373.

29. McAuliffe v. New Bedford, 155 Mass. 216 (1892) (1891–1892).

30. City of Newton v. Perry, 163 Mass. 321 (1895).

31. Ryalls v. Mechanics Mills, 150 Mass. 194 (1889–1890).

32. Commonwealth v. Perry, 155 Mass. 117, 123 (1891).

33. Holmes wrote Pollock concerning this same case on April 15, 1892, "This morning I must prepare to give my opinion to the legislature whether they can authorize municipal wood and coal yards—a step toward Communism. I am likely to be in the minority and to think that they can. . . ." *Holmes-Pollock Letters*, I, 42.

34. Vegelahn v. Guntner, 167 Mass. 92, 104 (1896).

35. Plant v. Woods, 176 Mass. 492, 504 (1900).

36. 155 Mass. 609 (1891–1892).

37. In re Municipal Suffrage to Women, 160 Mass. 586, 594 (1894).

38. Commonwealth v. Davis, 162 Mass. 510 (1895).

39. Holmes to Pollock, Jan. 20, 1893, *Holmes-Pollock Letters*, I, 44.

40. Holmes to Pollock, April 2, 1894, ibid., I, 51.

41. Holmes to Pollock, Jan. 20, 1893, ibid., I, 44.

42. Holmes, "The Profession of Law," *The Holmes Reader*, p. 67.

43. Ibid.

44. Ibid., p. 68.

45. Holmes, "The Law," p. 62.

46. Holmes, "Early English Equity," *Collected Legal Papers*, p. 2.

47. Ibid., p. 4.

48. Ibid., p. 17.

49. Holmes, "Agency," ibid., p. 49, 50ff.

50. Holmes, "Agency II," ibid., p. 101.

51. Ibid., p. 114.

52. Holmes, "Privilege, Malice and Intent," ibid., p. 117.

53. Ibid., p. 118.

54. Ibid., p. 120.

55. Ibid.

56. Ibid., p. 126.

57. Ibid., p. 129.

58. Ibid.

59. Holmes, "Memorial Day," *Speeches*, pp. 1–12.

60. Ibid., p. 1.

61. Ibid., p. 3.

62. Ibid., p. 4.

63. Ibid., p. 6.

64. Ibid., p. 11.

65. Holmes, "The Use of Law Schools," *Collected Legal Papers*, pp. 36–37.

66. Ibid., p. 38.

67. Ibid.

68. Ibid., p. 41.

69. Ibid., p. 47.

70. Ibid., p. 48.

71. Edwin Arlington Robinson, "Lancelot," *Collected Poems* (New York, 1948), p. 415.

72. Holmes, "Brown University–Commencement," *Collected Legal Papers*, p. 166.

73. Holmes, "The Soldiers' Faith," *The Holmes Reader*, pp. 101–106.

74. Ibid., p. 102.

75. Ibid., p. 103.

76. Ibid., p. 104.

77. Ibid.

78. Ibid., p. 106.

79. Holmes, "The Path of the Law," *Collected Legal Papers*, pp. 167–202.

80. Ibid., p. 167.

81. Ibid., p. 169.

82. Ibid., p. 173.

83. Ibid., p. 187.

84. Ibid., p. 189.

85. Ibid., p. 202.

86. Holmes, "Law in Science and Science in Law," ibid., pp. 210–43.

87. Ibid., pp. 225–26.

88. Ibid., p. 233.

89. Ibid., p. 231.

90. Holmes, "Speech," ibid., pp. 244–49.

91. Ibid., p. 246.

92. Ibid., p. 247.

93. Ibid.

Chapter Five

1. Holmes to Pollock, Dec. 21, 1902, *Holmes-Pollock Letters*, I, 109.

2. Holmes to Pollock, Jan. 2, 1904, ibid., I, 115.

3. As G. Edward White has written, "progressives found Holmes an especially attractive and sympathetic judicial figure and contributed to the growth of his stature." For a useful discussion of Holmes and the Progressives see White, *The Rise and Fall of Justice Holmes,* 39 U. Chi. L. Rev., 55, 58 (1971–1972).

4. Coppage v. Kansas, 236 U.S. 1, 26 (1914).

5. Gompers v. United States, 233 U.S. 604, 610 (1913).

6. Northern Securities Company v. United States, 193 U.S. 197, 400 (1903).

7. Lochner v. New York, 198 U.S. 45, 74 (1905).

8. Otis v. Parker, 187 U.S. 606 (1902).

9. Missouri, Kansas & Texas Railway Co. v. May, 194 U.S. 267 (1903).

10. Holmes to Laski, July 28, 1916, *Holmes-Laski Letters,* I, 8.

11. Holmes to Laski, March 28, 1920, ibid., I, 254.

12. Missouri v. Holland, 252 U.S. 416 (1919).

13. *Ex parte* Indiana Transportation Company, 244 U.S. 456 (1917).

14. Hammer v. Dagenhart, 247 U.S. 251, 277 (1917).

15. Holmes to Pollock, March 7, 1909, *Holmes-Pollock Letters,* I, 152.

16. Holmes to Pollock, Oct. 21, 1895, ibid., I, 64.

17. Holmes to Pollock, Aug. 9, 1897, ibid., I, 77.

18. Holmes to Pollock, May 25, 1906, ibid., I, 123.

19. See Arthur F. Beringause, *Brooks Adams, A Biography* (New York, 1955), pp. 68ff. For an exceptionally perceptive appreciation of Holmes set in the larger intellectual framework of the times, see Rogat, *The Judge as Spectator,* 31 U Chi. L. Rev. 213 (1964).

20. David W. Noble, *The Paradoxes of Progressive Thought* (New York, 1958), gives a good account of the Progressive mind. Henry S. Commager, *The American Mind* (New Haven, Conn., 1950) places Holmes in useful relationship to the larger American mind; see especially pp. 381–90.

21. Roosevelt to Lodge, July 10, 1902, *The Letters of Theodore Roosevelt,* Elting E. Morison, et al., eds., 8 vols. (Cambridge, Mass., 1951–1954), III, 289.

22. 193 U.S. 197, 400 (1901).

23. 198 U.S. 45, 74 (1904).

24. 196 U.S. 375 (1904).

25. 200 U.S. 496 (1905).

26. 201 U.S. 562, 628 (1905).

27. 199 U.S. 401 (1903).
28. 206 U.S. 246 (1906).
29. 208 U.S. 161, 190 (1907).
30. 207 U.S. 463, 541 (1907).
31. 213 U.S. 138, 149 (1908).
32. 227 U.S. 308 (1913).
33. 216 U.S. 56, 75 (1909).
34. 215 U.S. 349, 370 (1909).
35. United States v. Winslow, 227 U.S. 202 (1913).
36. Dr. Miles Medical Company v. Park & Sons Company, 220 U.S. 373, 409 (1911).
37. 219 U.S. 104, 575 (1910).
38. 223 U.S. 655 (1911).
39. 229 U.S. 373 (1912).
40. 234 U.S. 216 (1913).
41. 233 U.S. 604 (1913).
42. 235 U.S. 522 (1914).
43. Brandeis to Thomas Watt Gregory, April 14, 1916, *Letters of Louis D. Brandeis,* Melvin I. Urofsky and David W. Levy, eds., 4 vols. (Albany, N.Y., 1971), IV, 165.
44. Brandeis to Alfred Brandeis, July 31, 1875, ibid., I, 45.
45. Brandeis to Holmes, Dec. 9, 1882, ibid., I, 65.
46. Brandeis to Holmes, Sept. 3, 1902, ibid., I, 207.
47. Holmes to Laski, Dec. 27, 1925, *Holmes-Laski Letters,* I, 810.
48. Holmes to Laski, Oct. 5, 1919, ibid., I, 212.
49. Southern Pacific Ry. v. Jensen, 244 U.S. 205, 218 (1916).
50. Wilson v. New, 243 U.S. 332 (1917).
51. Holmes, "Natural Law," *Harvard Law Review,* XXXII (1918), 40–44 passim.
52. Wilfred E. Rumble, *American Legal Realism* (Ithaca, N.Y., 1968), pp. 41–44. For detailed statements of Frank and Pound referred to in the text see Frank, *Are Judges Human? Part One: The Effect of Legal Thinking of the Assumptions that Judges Behave Like Human Beings,* 80 U. PA. L. REV. 17 (1931); Pound, *Fifty Years of Jurisprudence: IV Realist Schools,* 51 HARV. L. REV. 777 (1938). For a recent brief appraisal, see Lawrence M. Friedman, *A History of American Law* (New York, 1973), p. 544.

Chapter Six

1. Holmes to Pollock, Aug. 30, 1914, *Holmes-Pollock Letters,* I, 219.

2. Holmes to Pollock, Nov. 7, 1914, ibid., I, 222.

3. Holmes to Einstein, Oct. 12, 1914, *Holmes-Einstein Letters,* p. 100.

4. Holmes to Pollock, Dec. 29, 1915, *Holmes-Pollock Letters,* I, 229.

5. Holmes to Laski, June 9, 1917, *Holmes-Laski Letters,* I, 89–90.

6. Holmes to Pollock, Nov. 3, 1917, *Holmes-Pollock Letters,* I, 250.

7. Holmes to Pollock, Feb. 18, 1917, ibid., I, 244.

8. Schenck v. United States, 249 U.S. 47 (1918).

9. Holmes to Laski, Feb. 28, 1919, *Holmes-Laski Letters,* I, 186. Though another case was handed down that day (*Panama Railroad Co. v. Bosse*), Holmes probably had the Schenck case particularly in mind. The remark, whatever the exact reference, leaves no doubt as to Holmes's determination to pass judgments; see ibid, n. 2.

10. Frohwerk v. United States, 249 U.S. 204 (1918).

11. Debs v. United States, 249 U.S. 211 (1918). Regarding the Debs case, Holmes told Herbert Croly that "it was impossible to have a rational doubt about the law." Holmes to Croly, May 12, 1919, *Holmes-Laski Letters,* I, 203.

12. Holmes to Laski, March 16, 1919, ibid., I, 190; to Pollock, April 5, 1919, *Holmes-Pollock Letters,* II, 2.

13. Holmes to Pollock, Dec. 14, 1919, ibid., II, 32.

14. Abrams v. United States, 250 U.S. 616, 624 (1919).

15. Holmes to Pollock, Oct. 26, 1919, *Holmes-Pollock Letters,* II, 27.

16. Pierce v. United States, 252 U.S. 239 (1920). Holmes concurred with Brandeis.

17. Holmes to Pollock, Jan. 19, 1928, *Holmes-Pollock Letters,* II, 212.

18. Ibid., II, 212–13.

19. American Bank & Trust v. Federal Bank, 256 U.S. 350, 358 (1921).

20. Jackman v. Rosenbaum Co., 260 U.S. 22, 31 (1922).

21. Milwaukee Socialist Democratic Publishing Company v. Burleson, 255 U.S. 407, 437 (1920).

22. Leach v. Carlile, Postmaster, 258 U.S. 138, 140 (1921).

23. Silverthorne Lumber Company v. United States, 251 U.S. 385 (1920).

24. United States v. Sullivan, 274 U.S. 259 (1927).

25. Gitlow v. New York, 268 U.S. 652, 672 (1924).

26. Holmes to Laski, June 24, 1925, *Holmes-Laski Letters*, I, 752.

27. Gitlow v. New York.

28. Olmstead v. United States, 276 U.S. 287, 293 (1927), Holmes wrote to Pollock that he agreed with all that Brandeis said in his dissent; Holmes to Pollock, June 28, 1920, *Holmes-Pollock Letters*, II, 222.

29. United States v. Schwimmer, 279 U.S. 644, 653 (1928).

30. Holmes to Laski, Aug. 23, 1929, *Holmes-Laski Letters*, II, 1177.

31. Holmes to Laski, June 15, 1929, ibid., II, 1158.

32. Holmes to Laski, Dec. 3, 1918, *Holmes-Laski Letters*, I, 176.

33. Holmes to Laski, Dec. 26, 1931, ibid., II, 1347.

34. Holmes to Brandeis, April 20, 1919, quoted in Alpheus Mason, *Brandeis: A Free Man's Life* (New York, 1946), p. 574. For a full discussion of the contribution of Holmes and Brandeis together, see Samuel J. Konefsky, *The Legacy of Holmes and Brandeis* (New York, 1956).

35. Bartels v. Iowa, 262 U.S. 404, 412 (1922).

36. Pennsylvania Coal Company v. Mahon, 260 U.S. 393 (1922). Holmes justified his position to Pollock pretty much as follows: as the owner of residences purchased only the surface rights and no more, he cannot arbitrarily enlarge his claim. Holmes to Pollock, Dec. 31, 1922, *Holmes-Pollock Letters*, II, 109.

37. United States v. United States Steel Corporation, 251 U.S. 417 (1920).

38. Wallace v. Himes, 253 U.S. 66 (1920). See also Eureka Pipe Line Company v. Halloman, 257 U.S. 265 (1921), wherein Holmes stated, "As has been repeated many times, interstate commerce is a practical conception. . . ."

39. Erie Railroad Company v. Public Utility Commissioners, 254 U.S. 394 (1921).

40. American Column v. United States, 257 U.S. 377, 412 (1921).

41. Truax v. Corrigan, 257 U.S. 312, 343 (1921).

42. Holmes to Laski, Dec. 22, 1921, *Holmes-Laski Letters*, I, 390.

43. Truax v. Corrigan.

44. Adkins v. Children's Hospital, 261 U.S. 525, 567 (1922).

45. Holmes to Laski, April 14, 1923, *Holmes-Laski Letters*, I, 495.

46. Myers v. United States, 272 U.S. 52, 77 (1926).

47. Springer v. Philippine Islands, 277 U.S. 189, 209 (1927).

48. Myers v. United States.

49. Moore v. Dempsey, 261 U.S. 86 (1923).

50. Nixon v. Herndon, 273 U.S. 536 (1927).

51. Baldwin v. Missouri, 281 U.S. 586, 595 (1930).

52. Bowen, p. 410. 44 HARV. L. REV. (1931) was dedicated to Holmes on the occasion of his ninetieth birthday. The most useful of the pieces included in this chorus of laudation are Cardozo, *Mr. Justice Holmes*, 682; Pound, *The Call for a Realist Jurisprudence*, 697; and Plucknett, *Holmes, The Historian*, 712. In addition, there is a complete list of all opinions delivered by Holmes while on the Massachusetts Supreme Court, pp. 799–819, and while on the United States Supreme Court, pp. 820–27.

Chapter Seven

1. The literature of the controversy is extensive. Perhaps the two most clearcut statements of praise and condemnation are Wyzanski, *The Democracy of Justice Holmes*, 7 VAND. L. REV. 311 (1954), and McKinnon, *The Secret of Mr. Justice Holmes, An Analysis*, 36 AM. B. A. J. 261 (1950). See the Selected Bibliography for further sources.

2. Howe, *The Positivism of Mr. Justice Holmes*, 64 HARV. L. REV. 529 (1951); Hart, *Holmes' Positivism—An Addendum*, id., 929; Howe, *A Brief Rejoinder*, id., 937. This exchange, while illuminating, is inconclusive as a debate. Francis Biddle, *Justice Holmes, Natural Law and the Supreme Court* (New York, 1961), deals with the overall controversy with an almost Holmesian detachment. See Chapter 2, "The Attacks on Justice Holmes," pp. 29–49. For a useful summary of the controversy see David H. Burton, ed., *Oliver Wendell Holmes, Jr., What Manner of Liberal?* (Huntington, N.Y., 1979).

3. While the full range of the Holmes literature bears directly or indirectly on the theme of this chapter, several particular discussions seem especially relevant. Among these are Felix Frankfurter, "Property and Society," pp. 43–73, and "Civil Liberties and the Individual," pp. 74–87; and John Dewey, "Justice Holmes and the Liberal Mind," pp. 33–45 in *Mr. Justice Holmes*. See as well Felix Frankfurter, *Mr. Justice Holmes and the Supreme Court* (Cambridge, Mass., 1961).

4. Quoted in Howe, *The Shaping Years*, p. 222.

5. 273 U.S. 418, 445 (1927).

6. Holmes to Dr. Wu, July 21, 1925, *Justice Holmes to Dr. Wu: An Intimate Correspondence, 1921–1932* (New York, n.d.), p. 31.

7. Holmes, "Law and the Court," *Collected Legal Papers*, p. 295.

8. Ibid.

9. Holmes, *Natural Law*, 32 Harv. L. Rev. 40, 40 (1918).

10. Felix Frankfurter, "Mr. Justice Holmes and the Constitution," *Mr. Justice Holmes*, p. 60.

11. Adkins v. Children's Hospital, 261 U.S. 525 (1922).

12. Holmes to Sheehan, Dec. 15, 1912, *Holmes-Sheehan Correspondence*, p. 56.

13. Francis Biddle, *Mr. Justice Holmes* (New York, 1941), p. 7.

14. Holmes to Sheehan, Dec. 15, 1912, *Holmes-Sheehan Correspondence*, p. 56.

15. Holmes to Pollock, April 5, 1932, *Holmes-Pollock Letters*, II, 307.

16. Holmes to Pollock, Dec. 11, 1928, ibid., II, 234.

Selected Bibliography

PRIMARY SOURCES

1. Books (including edited collections of Holmes's writings)

HOLMES, OLIVER WENDELL, JR., ed. *Kent's Commentaries*, 12th edition. Boston: Little, Brown and Company, 1873. An important source of Holmes's earliest attempts to give the law a pragmatic inflection.

————. *The Common Law*. Boston: Little, Brown and Company, 1881. It has had several editions, including one in paper published by Little, Brown in 1963, containing an excellent introduction by Mark deW. Howe.

————. *Speeches*. Boston: Little, Brown and Company, 1913, 1934. Contains Holmes's most important addresses.

————. *Collected Legal Papers*. New York: Harcourt, Brace and Howe, 1920. Includes significant writings on the law, apart from judicial opinions.

————. "Plato," *University Quarterly* II: 1 (Oct. 1860): 205–17. Not available in the various collections and deserves special notice.

HOWE, MARK DEW., ed. *Touched With Fire*. Cambridge, Mass.: Harvard Univ. Press, 1947. Holmes's Civil War letters and portions of a diary.

————, ed. *The Occasional Speeches of Justice Oliver Wendell Holmes*. Cambridge, Mass.: Harvard Univ. Press, 1962. Oddments, but indicative of the range of Holmes's mind.

LERNER, MAX, ed. *The Mind and Faith of Justice Holmes*. Boston: Little, Brown and Company, 1943. Both a comprehensive and a judicious selection of Holmes's work, with a masterful introduction by Lerner.

LIEF, ALFRED, ed. *The Dissenting Opinions of Mr. Justice Holmes*. New York: Vanguard Press, 1929. A useful compendium.

————, ed. *Representative Opinions of Mr. Justice Holmes*. New York: Vanguard Press, 1931. Contains excerpts from both state and federal cases.

SHRIVER, HARRY C., ed. *Justice Oliver Wendell Holmes, His Book*

Notices and Uncollected Letters and Papers. New York: Central Book Co., 1936. Some interesting fragments of Holmes's writings.

2. Letters

BURTON, DAVID H., ed. *Holmes-Sheehan Correspondence*. Port Washington, N.Y.: Kennikat Press Corp., 1977. Reveals a kindly Holmes not evident from other published sources.

COHEN, FELIX, ed. "The Holmes-Cohen Correspondence," *Journal of the History of Ideas* IX: 1 (Jan. 1948): 3–51. Rarefied philosophical talk marked by the humor and humility of the correspondents.

HOWE, MARK DEW., ed. *The Holmes-Pollock Letters*, 2 vols. Cambridge, Mass.: Harvard Univ. Press, 1941. Rich in legal and philosophical detail.

————, ed. *Holmes-Laski Letters*, 2 vols. Cambridge, Mass., Harvard Univ. Press, 1953. Holmes at his most candid.

PEABODY, JAMES B., ed. *Holmes-Einstein Letters*. London: Macmillan, 1964. An exchange noted for its civilized commentary.

WU, JOHN, ed. *Justice Holmes to Dr. Wu: An Intimate Correspondence*. New York: Central Book Company, 1947. Letters concerned mostly with the philosophy of law.

SECONDARY SOURCES

1. Books Dealing with Holmes in Particular

BENT, SILAS. *Justice Oliver Wendell Holmes*. New York: Vanguard Press, 1932. Comprehensive and critical, and still useful despite its early date.

BIDDLE, FRANCIS B. *Mr. Justice Holmes*. New York: Scribners Sons, 1942. More a sketch and a personal memoir than a biography.

————. *Mr. Justice Holmes, The Natural Law and the Supreme Court*. New York: Macmillan, 1961. Largely a defense of Holmes against his critics.

BOWEN, CATHERINE D. *Yankee from Olympus*. Boston: Little, Brown and Company, 1944. A hybrid of scholarship and popular writing, done with great sympathy for Holmes.

BURTON, DAVID H., ed. *Oliver Wendell Holmes, Jr., What Manner of Liberal?* Huntington, N.Y.: Krieger Publishing Company, 1979. Investigates the nature of Holmes's judicial outlook.

FRANKFURTER, FELIX, ed. *Mr. Justice Holmes*. New York: Coward-

McCann, 1931. Includes essays by John Dewey Cardozo, and
Morris R. Cohen.

————. *Mr. Justice Holmes and the Supreme Court.* Cambridge,
Mass.: Harvard Univ. Press, 1961. A disciple of Holmes evalu-
ates his work.

HOWE, MARK DEW. *Oliver Wendell Holmes The Shaping Years
1841–1870.* Cambridge, Mass.: Harvard Univ. Press, 1957; *The
Proving Years 1870–1882.* Cambridge, Mass.: Harvard Univ.
Press, 1963. The first two volumes of a projected definitive
biography, completed before Howe's death; scholarly, erudite,
and immensely readable; indispensable for coming to know the
young Holmes.

HURST, JAMES W. *Justice Holmes and Legal History.* New York:
Macmillan, 1964. A specialized approach by a first-rate scholar.

MARKE, JULIUS, ed. *The Holmes Reader.* Dobbs Ferry, N.Y.: Oceana
Publications, 1964. A collection of writings and evaluations con-
stituting a handy reference book.

2. Books in Which Holmes Receives Important Consideration

BERINGAUSE, ARTHUR F. *Brooks Adams, A Biography.* New York:
Alfred A. Knopf, 1955. Speaks of the overall influence of a
fellow Brahmin.

BOLLER, PAUL F. *American Thought in Transition.* Chicago: Rand
McNally, 1969. A straightforward account of Holmes in history.

COMMAGER, HENRY S. *The American Mind.* New Haven and London:
Yale Univ. Press, 1950. A standard treatment.

CURTI, MERLE. *The Growth of American Thought.* New York: Harper
and Row, 1964. Places Holmes in the larger context of American intellectual history.

GABRIEL, RALPH H. *The Course of American Democratic Thought.*
New York: Ronald Press, 1956. Treats Holmes critically.

GILMORE, GRANT. *The Ages of American Law.* New Haven and
London: Yale Univ. Press, 1977. Nonsentimental assessment.

KONEFSKY, SAMUEL J. *The Legacy of Holmes and Brandeis.* New
York: Macmillan, 1956. Sees the two jurists in a mutually
nourishing relationship.

MASON, ALPHEUS. *Brandeis, A Free Man's Life.* New York: Viking
Press, 1946. Good perspective on Holmes.

NOONAN, JOHN T. *Persons and Masks of the Law.* New York: Farrar,
Straus, and Giroux, 1976. Identifies Holmes with legal change.

WHITE, G. EDWARD. *The American Judicial Tradition.* New York:

Oxford Univ. Press, 1976. A deft summary of Holmes in history.
WIENER, PHILIP P. *Evolution and the Founders of Pragmatism.* Cambridge, Mass.: Harvard Univ. Press, 1949. A truly superior exposition of Holmes set in the large framework of the scientific revolution.

3. Periodical Literature, General

ALLEN, FRANCIS A. "Criminal Law," *University of Chicago Law Review* 31:2 (Winter 1964): 257–62. A good analysis of Holmes's treatment of criminal law in *The Common Law.*

BURTON, DAVID H. "The Intellectual Kinship of Oliver Wendell Holmes, Jr., Frederick E. Pollock, and Harold J. Laski." *Proceedings of the American Philosophical Society* 119:2 (April 16, 1975): 133–42. Explores common Anglo-American values.

————. "The Friendship of Justice Holmes and Canon Sheehan," *Harvard Library Bulletin* XXV:2 (April 1977): 155–69. Demonstrates the chemistry of friendship.

————. "Mr. Justice Holmes in England, 1866," *History Today* 29 (May 1979): 304–309. Discusses Holmes's early fondness for things English.

FIECHTER, FREDERICK C., JR. "The Preparation of an American Aristocrat, *New England Quarterly* VI:1 (March 1933): 3–28. Excellent on the early life of Holmes.

FISCH, MAX H. "Justice Holmes, the Predictive Theory of Law, and Pragmatism," *Journal of Philosophy* 39:4 (Feb. 1962): 85–97. A closely reasoned statement of the impact of pragmatism on Holmes.

GARRATY, JOHN. "Holmes' Appointment to the United States Supreme Court," *New England Quarterly* XXII:3 (Sept. 1949): 291–303. A full account of what proved to be a momentous appointment.

GOLDSMITH, ARNOLD L. "Oliver Wendell Holmes, Father and Son," *Journal of Criminal Law, Criminology and Political Science* 48:4 (Nov-Dec. 1957): 394–98. A provocative view of the father-son conflict.

KALVEN, HARRY, JR. "Torts," *University of Chicago Law Review* 31:2 (Winter 1964): 263–87. An evaluation of Holmes on torts in *The Common Law.*

PLUCKNETT, THEODORE F. T. "Holmes, The Historian," *Harvard Law Review* XLIV:5 (March 1931): 820–27. An excellent brief account of Holmes's use of history. (The March 1931 issue of the *Harvard Law Review* is devoted entirely to articles on

Holmes and gives a summary listing of all his opinions both as a state and federal judge.)

ROGAT, YOSAL. "The Judge as Spectator," *University of Chicago Law Review* 31:2 (Winter 1964): 213–56. Succeeds in putting Holmes into a larger intellectual setting.

SHARP, MALCOLM. "Contracts," *University of Chicago Law Review* 31:2 (Winter 1964): 268–78. Analyzes Holmes's treatment of contracts in *The Common Law.*

STECHOW, WOLFGANG. "Justice Holmes' Notes on Albert Dürer," *Journal of Aesthetics and Art Criticism* 7:2 (Dec. 1949): 119–24. Indicates how seriously Holmes took his work in woodcarving.

TOUSTER, SAUL. "In Search of Holmes from Within," *Vanderbilt Law Review* 19 (1964–1965): 438–72. One of the best appreciations of the role of the Civil War in the developing outlook of Holmes.

WHITE, G. EDWARD. "The Rise and Fall of Justice Holmes," *University of Chicago Law Review* 39:1 (1971–1972): 55–77. Thoughtful discussion of the "vogue" of Justice Holmes.

4. Periodical Literature Pertaining to Liberal/Conservative Controversy

BERNSTEIN, IRVING. "The Conservative Mr. Justice Holmes," *New England Quarterly* 23:4 (Dec. 1950): 435–52. Considerable evidence in support of a conservative interpretation while noting Holmes's liberal side.

BOORSTIN, DANIEL J. "The Elusiveness of Mr. Justice Holmes," *New England Quarterly* 14:3 (Sept. 1941): 478–87. Traces Holmes's elusiveness back to the struggle between pragmatism and mysticism, which was part of his intellectual growth.

DAVIS, H. B. "End of the Holmes Tradition," *University of Kansas City Law Review* 19 (1950–1951): 53–65. Largely descriptive.

FORD, JOHN C. "The Fundamentals of Holmes' Juristic Philosophy," *Fordham Law Review* 9:4 (Nov. 1942): 255–78. Accuses Holmes of a "complete divorce" of the legal and social orders, viewing this as a result of Holmes's denial of a personal God.

GREEN, NATHAN. "Mr. Justice Holmes and the Age of Man," *Wayne Law Review* 6:3 (Summer 1960): 394–412. A model of balanced discussion.

GREGG, PAUL L. "The Pragmatism of Mr. Justice Holmes," *Georgetown Law Journal* 31:3 (March 1943): 262–95. Charges Holmes with paving the way for a totalitarian form of government in America by popularizing a pragmatic philosophy.

HAMILTON, WALTON H. "On Dating Mr. Justice Holmes," *University of Chicago Law Review* 9:1 (Dec. 1941): 1–29. Indicates that the shining reputation Holmes had enjoyed should be critically viewed.

HART, HENRY M. "Holmes' Positivism—An Addendum," *Harvard Law Review* 64:4 (Feb. 1951): 929–37. Offers a challenging definition of Holmes's positivism.

HOWE, MARK DEW. "The Positivism of Mr. Justice Holmes," *Harvard Law Review* 64:4 (Feb. 1951): 529–46. Speaks glowingly of Holmes's philosophy, by whatever name.

————. "Brief Rejoinder," *Harvard Law Review* 64:4 (Feb. 1951): 937–39. Seeks to add a last word to an ongoing debate.

LASKI, HAROLD J. "The Political Philosophy of Mr. Justice Holmes," *Yale Law Journal* 40:5 (March 1931): 683–95. Makes a clear-cut statement of Holmes's public mind.

LUCEY, FRANCIS E. "Natural Law and American Legal Realism," *Georgetown Law Journal* 30:6 (April 1942) 493–533. Castigates Holmes for his failure to preserve a respect for moral rights in law and society.

————. "Holmes-Liberal-Humanitarian-Believer in Democracy?" *Georgetown Law Journal* 39:4 (May 1951): 523–662. An all-out attack, likening Holmes to Hitler.

McKINNON, HAROLD R. "The Secret of Mr. Justice Holmes: An Analysis," *American Bar Association Journal* 36 (April 1950): 261–64, 342–46. Highly skeptical of Holmes's liberalism.

PALMER, BEN W. "Hobbes, Holmes, Hitler," *American Bar Association Journal* 31 (November 1945): 569–73. Treats Holmes as part of a sinister pattern.

RODELL, FRED. "Holmes and His Hecklers," *Progressive* 15:4 (April 1951): 9–11. Polemical.

WYZANSKI, CHARLES E. "The Democracy of Justice Holmes," *Vanderbilt Law Review* 7 (April 1954): 311–23. Praises Holmes for his defense of popular government, civil liberties, and the dignity of man.

YNTEMA, HESSEL E. "Mr. Justice Holmes' View of Legal Science," *Yale Law Journal* 40:5 (March 1931): 683–95. Underscores the limits of Holmes's legal philosophy.

Index

167